'This is a book full of insight and anecdote, gracefully combined both to engage us and lead us forward in our life's pilgrimage with Jesus.'
Cardinal Vincent Nichols, Archbishop of Westminster

'This book is the perfect antidote to the stress and commercialism of our preparations for Christmas. Here is simple but satisfying food for prayer and reflection, shot through with personal stories and enlivened by a deep faith. This is soul food on which all can feed.'
Sir Philip Mawer, Canon Provincial of York

'For those of us who find mornings difficult, the last thing we want is someone shouting to wake us up. More helpful is a hot invigorating drink! This delightfully written book does not shout at you to wake up, clean up, feed up or grow up. Rather, it stimulates and motivates, engaging intellect and heart, Bible and tradition. The Archbishop brings Advent to life, injecting hope into despair, urgency into complacency, and demonstrating God at work in the world.'
David Wilkinson, Principal, St John's College, Durham

'In a book packed with helpful biblical readings and inspiring personal stories, Archbishop Sentamu encourages us – and challenges us – to wake up, clean up, feed up and grow up in Advent. Here is an Advent Calendar to open daily, with mounting joy and expectation, as we prepare for Christmas.'
Jane Williams, Assistant Dean, St Mellitus College, London

Dedicated to Her Majesty Queen Elizabeth II:
with deep gratitude and thanksgiving for her
inspiring Christmas reflections.
(I have listened to them all, as
broadcast in real time, from 1953.)

John SENTAMU

Wake Up to Advent!*

spck

First published in Great Britain in 2019

Society for Promoting Christian Knowledge
36 Causton Street
London SW1P 4ST
www.spck.org.uk

British Library Cataloguing-in-Publication Data
A catalogue record for this book is available from the British Library

ISBN 978–0–281–08354–1
eBook ISBN 978–0–281–08353–4

1 3 5 7 9 10 8 6 4 2

Typeset by The Book Guild Ltd, Leicester
Printed in Great Britain by Jellyfish Print Solutions

eBook by The Book Guild Ltd, Leicester

Produced on paper from sustainable forests

CONTENTS

Contents

ABOUT THE AUTHOR

Dr John Sentamu practised law in Uganda before he came to the UK in 1974. He was ordained deacon and priest in 1979. Following ordination, he was Assistant Chaplain at Selwyn College, Cambridge, after which he was Assistant Curate at St Andrew's, Ham, and Chaplain at Latchmere House Remand Centre. After serving as Assistant Curate at St Saviour's and St Paul's, Herne Hill, Dr Sentamu was Vicar of Holy Trinity and St Matthias, Tulse Hill, from 1983 to 1996. He was appointed Bishop of Stepney in 1996, then Bishop of Birmingham in 2002 and, latterly, Archbishop of York in 2005. He is Primate of England and Metropolitan, a member of the House of Lords and a Privy Councillor.

FOREWORD

A reader of the Archbishop of York's Advent book is being asked to do something rather unusual. This is not the kind of book which those who still read books today are likely to be familiar with. It is not a book of entertainment or imagination, and neither is it a book of information. It is not even a book of argument, marshalling facts and reasons to persuade us of a conclusion. The author has quite different aims from these, and the reader must decide at the beginning that what he hopes to accomplish is worth cooperating with. We might call it a book of 'formation' – a book to help us to *exist* more authentically as God has called us to exist.

It is very simple to read *through* but difficult to read *well*.

In the first place, *Wake Up to Advent!* is addressed to anybody and everybody. It is not written for the special group of those who will understand the questions or who have the right interests to engage with it. It invites us to rediscover ourselves as part of a mixed audience of all backgrounds and interests, who share those key interests and concerns common to all human beings: how to live and die; how to form and execute purposes; how to overcome failure; how to believe in themselves, other people and God.

In the second place, it must be read slowly – just two or three pages on each of the 25 days from Advent to

Christmas. Of course, the content can be thrown off in a moment, but then the book might as well be thrown away. It has to be allowed to penetrate our skin. Its stories need to haunt our minds, its claims allowed to irritate, excite and prompt new questions. One might even describe it as half a book, the other half being what the reader has to contribute in between times, while not actually reading it.

In the third place, it introduces the author to us personally. This is a book stamped with one man's mind and character. The autobiographical references are few but, as we read his book, we come to know him. We are invited to share his reflections in Advent as we might be invited to share his home. We would not expose ourselves in that way to just anybody. But John Sentamu is someone with a claim on our attention, and not merely because he holds a position of ancient dignity. He has brought to his role an integrity tempered like steel in his own struggles for life, justice and joy. An exceptional man with an exceptional right to our interest when he talks about what it takes to live.

He draws our attention to a reality we usually lose sight of because it looms so large that we cannot look straight at it – the future. It is comparatively easy to think about the past, especially when we think mainly of what others have done, and to luxuriate in strong views of approval and disapproval. It is more difficult to think about what we ourselves have done because we quickly become defensive; yet, if we are honest, we can tell of our own past truthfully, too. Yet the future is a blank page on which imagination projects a thousand unreal and incompatible fantasies and fears. Except when we narrow our gaze to a well-defined project and think only of ways and means, we find it almost impossible to *conceive* of the future, even though we live facing it all the time. But to be responsible for ourselves means preparing ourselves for the tasks of living, even though we do not know what they will be like. In Advent, Christians face this challenge by reflecting on the theme of preparation. The author helps us to learn self-preparation, taking us through the steps that make us attentive and ready actors in the world: hope, expectancy, confidence, awareness of what has been done for us and what we can count on. He will help us to see the history in which we live as one in which God has prepared his way for us.

This is a book written out of the deep resources of the Christian belief that responsibility for oneself is closely tied to responsibility before God. Yet the reader who approaches the book without sharing that faith may still discover how its questions and challenges belong to every human being. To attend to what is involved in living in the world teaches us to ask about the love that moves all things and has power to renew them. And even if that love is still a question mark, not a certainty, attending to its claims can only make us more truly human.

Oliver O'Donovan
Professor Emeritus, Christian Ethics
and Practical Theology
University of Edinburgh

COPYRIGHT ACKNOWLEDGEMENTS

INTRODUCTION

Each year, at this time – the beginning of the Church's year – we find ourselves facing in two directions. We look back, reflecting and rejoicing in the story of Christ's first coming to earth to be Emmanuel, God with us. We look forward, with hope and godly fear, to his glorious return: the Second Coming of Our Lord.

The season of Advent is given to us so that we can realign our compass to direct us on the right path. This is our New Year of the Church, when we ponder and renew our commitment, and our understanding of Christ's gracious invitation to us. How can we be ready? How should we prepare to celebrate both the anniversary of his wonderful birth, and the promise of his glorious return?

Last Sunday – the last Sunday before Advent – is traditionally known as 'Stir-up Sunday', a name which derives from the Collect for the day in the Book of Common Prayer – 'Stir up, we beseech thee, O Lord, the wills of thy faithful people; that they, plenteously bringing forth the fruit of good works, may of thee be plenteously rewarded.'

Over the years, the followers of Jesus have accepted its challenge to their trusting response and active commitment to serving God and one another. At the same time, the cooks in the congregation have taken it as a reminder that it's time to make their Christmas cakes. The making of a Christmas cake is a significant activity at this time. We begin it early – before the beginning of the Advent season – because it needs time to mature and develop its richest flavour. It brings together one of the largest lists of ingredients of any cake we're likely to make. It involves care in measuring, soaking, stirring, beating all the elements together. And it is significant that the final stirring is traditionally done by all the family members. It is a community activity and a community commitment if the best mix is to be achieved.

Then, when our wills have been stirred, and our love, faith and hope begin their slow maturing within us, we are ready to begin on our Advent journey.

WEEK 1: WAKE UP!

Collect for the First Sunday of Advent

Almighty God, give us grace to cast away the works of darkness and to put on the armour of light, now in the time of this mortal life, in which your Son Jesus Christ came to us in great humility; that on the last day, when he shall come again in his glorious majesty to judge the living and the dead, we may rise to the life immortal, through him who is alive and reigns with you in the unity of the Holy Spirit, one God, now and for ever.

The images and symbolism I want to use in this book are found in this prayer. They are the images of someone awaking from sleep and getting ready for the life of the day. Having stirred from our slumber, we are now ready to *Wake Up, Clean Up, Feed Up* and *Grow Up*. These are easy tasks to remember – we perform them each morning as we greet the new day. In this book, we look at how Jesus himself encouraged his disciples, how he encourages us to *Wake Up, Clean Up, Feed Up* and *Grow Up*. Then we shall be ready to remember and celebrate his blessed birth and look forward with confidence to his return.

Advent is a gift which we should unwrap carefully and humbly. Each day we discover a new layer of God's revelation to us. These days, the children's party game, pass-the-parcel, contains a gift in every layer and not just a big gift in the final unwrapping. This Advent, may we make God's gift to us, Jesus Christ, visible together.

Beginning this Advent Sunday, with the stirring words of the Apostle Paul to the Romans, let us wake up to Advent day-by-day through the readings, reflections and prayers of this book.

ADVENT SUNDAY

The Sleep of Darkness (Romans 13.11–14)

[11]Always remember that this is the hour of crisis: it is high time for you to wake out of sleep, for deliverance is nearer to us now than it was when first we believed. [12]It is far on in the night; day is near. Let us therefore throw off the deeds of darkness and put on the armour of light … [14]Let Christ Jesus himself be the armour that you wear; give your unspiritual nature no opportunity to satisfy its desires.

Each day of the year, as we say the opening prayer of Morning Prayer, we echo these words from the Letter to the Romans: 'The night has passed, and the day lies open before us; let us pray with one heart and mind.'

It is a wonderful way to begin the day. A welcome to the light; glad anticipation of all that awaits us in the day, and a readiness to pray for help and guidance in all that we do.

As we go through Advent, during the darkest weeks of the year (in the Northern Hemisphere), the images of darkness and light are constantly with us. This morning we will be lighting the first of our Advent candles, and each Sunday over the next four weeks, as we light the next candle, we shall be bringing more light into our lives. Then on Christmas Day, with the lighting of the fifth candle, we celebrate the Light of the World which came down at Christmas, and we look forward to the time that will come when there will be no more darkness.

What wakes you up in the morning? Is it a child bouncing in to your room at 6 a.m., or a partner kindly bringing you a cup of tea? Is it the shrill beeping of your alarm clock, or a flatmate flinging open the curtains and dripping cold water on your face?

However we wake up, there comes a time when 'the night has passed and the day lies open before us' and we have to emerge from the comfort of our darkened room and our cosy duvet.

In the same way, there comes a time, says the Apostle Paul, when we must wake from our spiritual darkness. When we need to open our eyes and see what time it is – each morning we wake up is one day closer to the day of Salvation, one day nearer our Lord's return.

What will Christ find when the light of that glorious second coming shines on our lives? Are we ready for what will be revealed about the way we've been living, or will we groan and pull the covers back over our head, preferring to return to the darkness?

If we prefer to remain creatures of the night, indulging in the habits of the night, we might find that we sleep through the day – and the danger is that we will also sleep through The Day of the Lord.

Sometimes it can be a relief to wake up. Our sleep may be disturbed by the dreams, fantasies and, sometimes, the nightmares of the darkness, and the bright reality of the day brings relief and hope. How often do we find that the troubles that have made us toss and turn during the night clear like morning mist and no longer frighten us as dawn comes? Even when troubles remain, the day gives us energy and a clear mind to tackle them.

What are we waking up to? What are the promises of the Day? As followers of Jesus Christ, we awake to a new order, the new life of the Kingdom which has been brought in by the resurrection of our Lord Jesus Christ. That is

3

something to get us up in the morning. That is something which gives us a new perspective, a new plan of action. The plan of action involves throwing off our night-time selves, and finding an alternative, appropriate for a new dawn, preparing to live with a new mind-set, 'give your unspiritual nature no opportunity to satisfy its desires,' the Apostle Paul says (Romans 13.14).

Are you one of those well-organized people who prepares what you will wear the night before? Is your outfit clean, ironed and hanging ready for you to put on, your shoes shiny and gleaming; or are you someone who rummages around in the wash basket for something that you can just about get away with one more time? Perhaps you're somewhere in between? Wherever you are on that spectrum, it's likely that you will be properly dressed before you go out. You won't be just pottering out in your pyjamas.

You may know the phrase 'clothes make the man'. Like so many well-known phrases which aren't from the Bible, it is from Shakespeare – from *Hamlet*. Polonius is advising his son Laertes about how to conduct himself when he goes off to Paris. In the middle of his speech he says, 'Costly thy habit as thy purse can buy, But not express'd in fancy; rich, not gaudy; For the apparel oft proclaims the man ...' (*Hamlet,* Act I, Scene III).

In other words: 'Spend all you can afford on clothes, but make sure they're quality, not flashy, since clothes make the man.'

It is advice which is also given by work psychologists. Dress smartly and you will feel smart – both in appearance and ability. It's amazing how putting on a smart outfit and shining your shoes helps you feel fit and ready for action.

What you choose to wear will have to stand you in good stead for whatever life will throw at you.

As morning people, 'children of light', we need to dress accordingly.

The Apostle Paul's advice for our comprehensive makeover is to *put on the Lord Jesus Christ*. We're not just going to put on an outward show, we're going to inhabit the characteristics of Jesus Christ. We're going to be living in him, and he in us. He will be our armour of light, protecting us against the deeds and desires of darkness and indicating to all those around that we are people who know where we are going.

When you dress in this way, you will find that your behaviour changes to match your outfit.

My grandchildren love to dress up, and when they put on grand cloaks or fancy headdresses, they become the princess, the hero, the doctor or the dancer. If we are as wholehearted as little children, we will find that when we put on Jesus Christ, we too become more like him.

Prayer

Lord Jesus Christ, may we remember this Advent that we are children of the light. May we wake up each day ready to take up the tasks of the day. And may our sleep be the restoring and health-giving rest that comes from tasks well done. Amen.

Reflection

This Advent, as we reflect on the coming of our Lord, let us look for a new way of living that will help us welcome the day, and make the best use of it. Let us think about

Advent alternatives to the pleasures and attractions of the present age, which may lead us back to darkness.

WEEK 1: MONDAY

The Sleep of Unawareness (1 Thessalonians 5.1–11)

> About dates and times, my friends, there is no need to write to you, [2]for you yourselves know perfectly well that the day of the Lord comes like a thief in the night … [6]And we must not sleep like the rest, but keep awake and sober … [11]Therefore encourage one another, build one another up – as indeed you do.

I don't know if the parents among you are already telling your children how many 'sleeps' it is until Christmas. Are they counting down the days on your Real Advent calendar, reading the story and enjoying the chocolate treats?

Unlike the shepherds, the wise men and all the other people living before that first Advent, and longing for the future coming of the Christ, we know the date of Christmas and we can count the days. We can enjoy the waiting without that sense of uncertainty we have about Christ's Second Advent.

The Thessalonian Christians had become obsessed about the timing of the Second Coming. They wanted to get it in their mind-diaries so they could fit it in to their plans. Many Christians in the centuries following have spent time and effort in trying to pin this event down, but that isn't what being ready and prepared means. It's not about scheduling Christ in, for some day in the future; it's about being on permanent alert.

The letter to the Thessalonians, written around AD 51, is actually the first letter the Apostle Paul wrote to the churches. Yet this question about the Second Coming must have featured in the list of 'Frequently Asked Questions' in the early days of the Church. As we saw yesterday, he needed to write the same warning to the Church in Rome, and later he wrote in similar terms to the Churches in Corinth.

When will Christ return? What should we look out for? What clues are there? It must also have been the question that the Apostles in the early church debated among themselves, and they would have remembered Jesus Christ's words in Matthew 24.42–44: '42Keep awake, then, for you do not know on what day your Lord will come. 43Remember, if the householder had known at what time of night the burglar was coming, he would have stayed awake and not let his house be broken into. 44Hold yourselves ready, therefore, because the Son of Man will come at the time you least expect him.'

The Apostle Paul had not been there when Jesus spoke these words, but it was clearly a much-discussed issue, because he uses almost the same words and imagery as Jesus when he spoke of the thief and the woman in labour pains.

We tend not to think about the crime statistics in Jesus Christ's time. We hear about the moral corruption of people in power, of the greed and dishonesty of tax collectors and, on one occasion, highway robbery on the road to Jericho, but thieves, apart from the ones crucified with Jesus, aren't much mentioned. Yet the concept of the thief in the night was obviously one that resonated with his hearers. Jesus Christ's warning to be prepared for the Day of the Lord arriving unexpectedly like a thief in the night was remembered and recorded by both Matthew and Luke. It is mentioned in three of the Apostle Paul's letters to various churches, and it is mentioned again in the book of Revelation. The fear and vulnerability we feel with the threat of our security being compromised and the things we hold valuable being taken from us is a powerful reminder of the need to be prepared and vigilant.

'Keep awake and sober' the Apostle Paul tells the Thessalonians. If the Day of the Lord comes unexpectedly, like a 'thief in the night', we need to be aware that the way we live might already be leading us to lose what's of virtue in us. You know this already, says the Apostle Paul. You don't need to be told again, but you *do* need to wake up. It was a message he needed to tell all the young churches he was in touch with.

The wake-up call that the Apostle Paul is giving the congregations of Rome and Thessalonica is a wake-up call not just for breakfast, but for the whole of their lives. It's not just someone saying 'Good Morning'. It's saying – Do you actually know what time it is? While you're asleep you can't think, you can't see, you can't act, you may be deceived into thinking dreams are the reality. Get your act together or you'll be sleepwalking into disaster – you'll miss the most important thing that will ever happen in your lives. It's time to wake up NOW! And *stay awake*!

Whatever you got up to last night – forget it and move on. That's not the person who needs to be going out in God's service this morning. The dark times are in the past. The grime of dissipation needs to be washed away and your mind and your will must turn towards the light.

How can we do this? As we read in the letter to the Romans yesterday, the best way of staying awake is to be properly prepared. Have the garments you will need ready for the day and laid out. Make sure your heart is in the right place – clothe yourself in love and faith. Make sure your head – your thoughts – are protected with the hope of salvation. Then you are in a fit state to face whatever the day has in store, and nothing can daunt your spirit.

You may face nothing more dramatic than the usual work and challenges that work and life bring. Or this might actually be the day when the Lord comes in glory! Between one breath and the next.

Is this possibility a comfort or a threat?

If you are well-prepared, awake, properly dressed and among brothers and sisters, colleagues and friends who are all working for the same goal, the Apostle Paul's last sentences are the promise of joy. You are not facing The Day alone – you are in the loving company of the faithful, 'therefore encourage one another and build up each other, as indeed you are doing' (1 Thessalonians 5.11 NRSV).

Prayer

Holy Spirit, this Advent, shine your light of truth and love into our lives; break into our unconsciousness with the hope you set before us, and help us wake, and turn our lives towards the warmth of the One True Light, even Jesus Christ our Lord. Amen.

Reflection

In the dark we are people with impaired vision. We can't see the objects around us, we can't see colours or beauty. We may stumble in the wrong direction, we may be filled with fear, we may be unable to see the light at the end of the tunnel and so we may fall into the idea that there is no end to the tunnel, and no light. There are two things we can do – grumble and despair or hope and pray. Make the choice.

WEEK 1: TUESDAY

The Sleep of Unpreparedness (Matthew 25.1–13)

When the day comes, the kingdom of Heaven will be like this. There were ten girls, who took their lamps and went out to meet the bridegroom. [2]Five of them were foolish, and five prudent; [3]when the foolish ones took their lamps, they took no oil with them, [4]but the others took flasks of oil with their lamps … [13]Keep awake then; for you know neither the day nor the hour.

Everyone loves a wedding story. The fact that there's a whole wedding channel on television gives us a hint about the fascination many people feel about the drama and theatre that can surround a wedding. I'm sure the crowds of men and women in the time of Jesus were just as interested in the preparation and excitement of one of the most important traditional events in their lives.

I have officiated at many weddings, and was particularly delighted to be able to officiate at the weddings of our two children and our foster-son. We hosted receptions for the children in our garden. Our son's was a summer wedding, on a hot sunny August day; our daughter's was on 17 December in the middle of a snowstorm; our foster-son's wedding and reception were in hot Mombasa! All those who were preparing for these celebrations had to make sure that all the arrangements were in place – the service booklets, the clothes – sunhats in August, umbrellas and wellington boots in December! The chairs and tables, food, crockery, enough cool drinks for a hot August day; enough fan heaters for the marquee on a snowy December evening. And the cook – me – had two days to prepare the food. All the details needed to be in place to ensure happy and smooth-running events. In Mombasa the hotel did it all. My role was taking the service.

Wedding celebrations in Jesus Christ's day could last a week, and involved a number of different stages and activities – including processions, music and feasting.

Jesus tells a dramatic story full of human interest, anxiety and joy, as well as a message for the whole of our lives. A story of people waiting for the arrival of the longed-for bridegroom.

Advent is a time for reflecting on the reality of Christ's coming – not just the Christmas story which we know, but the wedding story when Christ returns to claim his bride, the Church.

When we read the Prophets' words about the coming Messiah, and even when we read the gospel stories of Christ's life with us on earth, there is still a lot of uncertainty, confusion and misunderstanding about what his advent will mean. Even the disciples don't quite understand the reality and promise contained until he has risen, ascended, and the Holy Spirit has come on the day of Pentecost.

Do we really believe that the Day could arrive at any time? How real is the Second Coming for us – the heavenly wedding banquet?

Like the bridesmaids in the story, we are in the bride's wedding party, awaiting the bridegroom. How are we filling our time? Are we ready for this Day? Have we given up, thinking he'll never arrive? Waiting is a real challenge to our character, and to the quality of our love. Waiting requires trust, patience, obedience, hope and determination. It also requires energy to remain focused in spite of the distractions of anxiety or the weariness of boredom. When will this waiting end?

We hear in the story that there's a delay – the dramatic tension is ratcheted up for Jesus' listeners. What happened? Has he changed his mind? What will happen?

Ever since Adam and Eve grew tired of obedience, we humans have struggled with the task of waiting faithfully for a master we don't see. Yet it can be done! A book of Mother Teresa's letters describes how, soon after responding to Christ's call to her 'to serve the poorest of the poor', she entered a time of darkness – lasting until her death – in which she experienced the absence of Jesus. Yet she never gave up her obedience and faith in that first call and continued to offer that faithful service which God required of her.

Today's passage outlines two ways of waiting – wise and foolish, obedient and careless ways. The girls in this story have only one task: to keep their lamps burning so that they can lead the bridegroom to the wedding banquet. Waiting, when we can't keep busy, is a real challenge to our concentration and focus. It's hard work for the mind. Some of the girls kept to the task; others were silly and careless. Perhaps they had found more exciting things to do than buying oil and keeping their lamps clean and trimmed and ready. 'We can always do that nearer the time', they might have said.

A story is told of a percussion player in an orchestra. They were to perform Ravel's *Bolero*, and had been rehearsing hard. The man's job was to strike the cymbals as a great climax at the end of the piece. If you have heard of Ravel's *Bolero*, you will know the same tune and the same rhythm are repeated throughout – 18 variations of the same melody, each played by different instruments. The percussion player had to listen very carefully and count the bars until his great moment came. One lapse of concentration, one brief shift of focus, and he lost count! He missed his entry and it was too late for his great finale. Perhaps he took his eyes off the conductor.

When we are waiting for Christ's coming, we need constantly to have our attention on our heavenly conductor; we need to be watching and following what the other parts are doing as they follow his direction. Watching, not with binoculars scanning the horizon, but delighting in contemplation of the Christ who is forever nearer to us than our breath.

Prayer

Heavenly Father, may we be ever ready to play our part, however small, when the moment comes, and may we hear Christ's call to us and always be ready to serve him to the end – especially the poor, the prisoner, the differently abled, the broken victims, in this year of Your Favour. Amen.

Reflection

This Advent, consider the image of the Church as the bridal party waiting for the bridegroom's arrival: a palpable community of the Holy Spirit. Do you believe the wedding is worth waiting for? In what ways do you think that you, as a body, and as individuals, are working at staying alert and focused?

WEEK 1: WEDNESDAY

The Sleep of Withdrawal (Matthew 26.36–46)

[36]Jesus then came with his disciples to a place called Gethsemane, and he said to them, 'Sit here while I go over there to pray.' [37]He took with him Peter and the two sons of Zebedee. Distress and anguish overwhelmed him, [38]and he said to them, 'My heart is ready to break with grief. Stop here, and stay awake with me.' [39]Then he went on a little farther, threw himself down, and prayed, 'My Father, if it is possible, let this cup pass me by. Yet not my will but yours.' [40]He came back to the disciples and found them asleep; and he said to Peter, 'What! Could none of you stay awake with me for one hour? [41]Stay awake, and pray that you may be spared the test. The spirit is willing, but the flesh is weak.' [42]He went away a second time and prayed: 'My Father, if it is not possible for this cup to pass me by without my drinking it, your will be done.' [43]He came again and found them asleep, for their eyes were heavy. [44]So he left them and went away again and prayed a third time, using the same words as before. [45]Then he came to the disciples and said to them, 'Still asleep? Still resting? The hour has come! The Son of Man is betrayed into the hands of sinners. [46]Up, let us go! The traitor is upon us.'

During my life I have had many occasions to watch and wait with people in times of trouble – sitting, often in silence, praying and watching. They may be lying ill in hospital; mourning the loss of a loved one; waiting for test results; they may be in prison, or struggling with difficult family relationships. Waking, watching and praying in solidarity with others is part of a priest's life. Yet it is also part of what every member of God's family is called to do as we love one another.

Perhaps I may share a personal family memory of such an experience. I remember staying with my mother, Ruth – in her room at Trinity Hospice, Clapham – dying from throat cancer, never leaving her side for seven days. She was the one person who had loved and cared for me as a baby who weighed only four pounds, and who was expected to die before reaching the age of five. Even then, there was no guarantee that I would reach the age of ten. Dr Billington, who brought me into the world, said to my mother, 'What Sentamu needs is to be loved all the time'. Her love would not let me go, and I stayed at her bedside till death parted us. 'There is nothing love cannot face: there is no limit to its faith, its hope, its endurance' (1 Corinthians 13.7). Our two children, Grace and Geoffrey, aged 15 and 10 at the time, said, 'Grandma is so peaceful. We haven't lost her: she has simply departed from us. We will see her!' The look on their faces was awe-inspiring.

Nevertheless, there are many reasons watching and waiting can be difficult. Entering into that dark night of people's lives can be a huge challenge to our own physical and spiritual strength. And we can see this same struggle in the disciples.

Jesus himself is facing the most dreadful challenge of his life. He is terrifyingly alone in the face of the implacable hostility and deadly plans, not only of the powers of the land, but also the evil of the spiritual realm. He needs to know that his friends are upholding him, that they 'are backing him up' both physically and spiritually. Yet he finds that they have already deserted him; they have retreated into sleep, the sleep of denial. For many people suffering from stress or mental trauma, sleep is an escape route when life is too hard.

Jesus does not condemn the disciples, and neither, of course, should we. How ready are we to engage completely in entering into the misery of others?

It is part of the role of clergy that we must be ready and willing to serve others in this way, but it is recognized by the Church that it is a hard calling. Every time I ordain deacons, priests and bishops, I say these words in the Ordination Service, 'You cannot bear the weight of this calling in your own strength, but only by the grace and power of God. Pray therefore that your heart may daily be enlarged and your understanding of the scriptures enlightened. Pray earnestly for the gift of the Holy Spirit.'

The congregation of friends and supporters is later asked if they are willing to pray for the ordinand, and all answer 'Yes'. I hope that all who read this book – deacons, priests, bishops and laypeople (the holy ones of God) – are staying awake to pray for the Holy Spirit's strength and guidance.

The disciples' spirit was willing; they knew Jesus needed them, they loved him and wanted to accompany him in his struggle; but the exhaustion which comes from fear and uncertainty overpowered them. Sometimes the power of darkness, which we encounter as we enter into the pain of others, can find a chink in our spiritual armour and overwhelm us. Journeying with others, and sharing their burdens, is not an easy service. Yet we must remember that we are not the centre of the universe. We are fallible people in whom the Holy Spirit lives. Like our Lord, we have to go lower, on our knees, to be the slaves of others. Stopping whatever we are doing to honour, worship and delight in God. And joining in the stream of intercessory prayer of Jesus Christ and the Holy Spirit, which they are forever offering to the Father – for you and me (Romans 8.26-27; Hebrews 7.24–25).

Sometimes, like Peter, we are buoyed up with the enthusiasm of the glorious gospel of love and service, and we feel that we are equal to anything; but when we have to enter the reality of taking up our cross, giving up our freedom, accepting rejection and unjust condemnation, we are daunted. Yes, we need to wake up to the fact that the flesh is weak, and to turn again to the whole armour of God to protect us if we want to be Christ to one another.

Because throughout human history, God has accompanied his people through pain and trouble. He is a God abounding in mercy, steadfast love and friendliness, who keeps faith and will never leave us. The pain and the trouble may not go away immediately or at all until we are with him in Glory, but he walks with us and upholds us. Jesus Christ who went so far as to die for us, assures us that he is with us to the end of the age. Let us not run away when we come face-to-face with friends who are suffering. Let us not glibly promise to pray and then fall into selfish forgetfulness.

We don't have to solve their problems, but may we offer our loving company to our brothers and sisters in Christ and to all who cross our path.

Jesus called his friends to be alongside him. He wasn't asking them to take action – in fact he rebuked Peter when he struck out at one of the guards who had come to arrest him. Jesus was asking for the disciples to be awake, to be waiting in solidarity with him. Why did they fail?

They failed to watch and pray for resilience. In Romans 13.14, as we read last Sunday, the followers of Jesus are encouraged to 'Let Christ Jesus himself be the armour that you wear; give your unspiritual nature no opportunity to satisfy its desires.' The disciples' flesh held sway because they did not quite understand that Jesus had invited them to keep watch, and not to take a rest.

Though the disciples were unable to offer him this service of love and loyalty, though they ran away, and Peter denied Jesus, they did not give up on him completely. They remained, watching for the dawn and the return of light to their lives. In contrast, Judas came to find Jesus in darkness, and after his betrayal he returned to the darkness, and never emerged again into the light. He succumbed to the powers of darkness which entered him and exacted a very high price. The temple of Mammon always demands a costly sacrifice for anyone who bows down to its altar.

Prayer

When we wake up we are often unaware of the challenges ahead of us. Father help us to remember to put on the Lord Jesus Christ so that we can go out into the day in his strength. Help us daily to go into God before we go out into the world. Amen.

Reflection

In the Garden of Gethsemane, the disciples had their last chance to be with Jesus, to 'share his sufferings' (Philippians 3.10), and be a strengthening presence. How often do we regret missed opportunities with friends and loved ones? How can we remain alert in solidarity with those who are suffering and not be tempted away by 'compassion fatigue'?

WEEK 1: THURSDAY

Waking to the Promise of Hope (Isaiah 52.1–3, 7–11)

Awake, awake, Zion, put on your strength; Jerusalem, Holy City, put on your splendid garments! ... ⁷How beautiful on the mountains are the feet of the herald, the bringer of good news, announcing deliverance, proclaiming to Zion, 'Your God has become king.' ⁸Your watchmen raise their voices and shout together in joy; for with their own eyes they see the Lord return to Zion.

The Book of Isaiah has two main themes; Chapters 1–39 speak mainly of God's judgment against Judah as the prophet issues a call to repentance and holiness. Chapters 40–66 contain God's message of forgiveness, consolation and hope, as God speaks through Isaiah, revealing his plan of blessing and salvation through the promised Messiah.

As we approach Christmas, we are also entering the season of *Messiah* concerts. It is part of our Christmas tradition – perhaps particularly in the north of England – for choirs in churches, town halls, concert halls and city squares to sing those glorious solos and choruses which lift our hearts with joy as we hear the promises about the coming Christ. The composer, Georg Friedrich Handel, took for his inspiration the words of hope from these chapters in the King James Version of the Book of Isaiah. 'Comfort ye, comfort ye, my people, saith your God ...' – the first words of Chapter 40 set the tone, and these words from Chapter 52 are found in the later solo, 'How beautiful are the feet of him that bringeth glad tidings of salvation that saith unto Sion, thy God reigneth! Break forth into joy! Glad tidings thy God reigneth' (Isaiah 52.7–9 KJV).

No wonder the prophet is calling to the people to awake and rejoice; no wonder the sentinels are singing for joy.

Wake up – it's good news, worth waking up for. Wake up and dress for a celebration; wake up and know that you are no longer a crushed and beaten people, but the free and indomitable beloved children of God.

Put on your garments of splendour (the whole armour of God); protect yourself from the harm the darkness of sin and temptation can do.

Those that wish you harm have no more power over you; dress confidently to show that you know your ransom is paid and the chains of oppression and bondage have been broken.

This, too, is our good news at Christmas. The coming of the Lord – the coming of light into our darkness – is the promise of a new world order, as it was for the people of Israel in exile. Christ's death and resurrection, and his promised return in glory, mean that we can live our lives now in the knowledge that our debts have been forgiven, and the chains of our subjugation to sin are destroyed for ever.

There is no better news to wake up for than the coming of Christ at Christmas and his return in Glory.

I remember, some time ago, reading the poem, 'How they brought the good news from Ghent to Aix' by Robert Browning. It describes the thrilling ride of three horsemen, dashing through the night from Ghent to Aix to take good news. The journey is long and fast. As morning breaks, one horse falls, dying of exhaustion, but the other two press on through the day, until a second horse stumbles and dies. The last labours on, battling thirst and fatigue, until the rider – seeing their goal within reach – throws off his coat, his holsters, his boots and finally his belt, to lighten the load on his gallant horse. When they finally make it to Aix the townspeople are full of praise and gladness and gratitude for the steadfast courage and dedication of those who brought the news.

We never learn, in the poem, what the good news was. Yet in Isaiah's poem it is clear that the good news that the messenger is bringing is the best news of all – the reign of God and salvation for his people.

So many countries across the world are suffering from oppression, brutality, fear and despair. The hope on people's faces when they look for news of peace, the joyful tears in the eyes of old and young when peace and rescue come, remind us to bless God for his gracious liberation.

This suffering and hope have continued down the centuries, from the time of Isaiah to the present day, and the stories from every age of hope and freedom resonate in our hearts.

On 5 December 1955, the Civil Rights bus boycott began in Montgomery, Alabama. It was inspired by a young black woman, Rosa Parks, who had refused to stand to allow a white man to take her seat. This was the beginning of a great movement of peaceful resistance in the face of the oppressive system of segregation and discrimination. Mrs Parks removed the chains of injustice from her neck and allowed a whole community to stand with her in the struggle. She made a decision to wake herself up from acquiescence and to wake others up to the injustice which subdued them.

Approximately 40,000 African-American bus riders – the majority of the city's bus riders – rose up and boycotted the system from 5 December. The next day, Revd Martin Luther King, Jr, the 26-year-old pastor of Montgomery's

Dexter Avenue Baptist Church, was elected to lead the Montgomery Improvement Association (MIA). The boycott lasted until 21 December the following year, when the buses were desegregated. However, the struggle continued for many more years. Martin Luther King's famous 'I have a dream' speech in 1963, eight years later, expressed the people's hope in the words of Isaiah 40: 'I have a dream that one day every valley shall be exalted, every hill and mountain shall be made low. The rough places will be made plain, and the crooked places will be made straight. And the Glory of the Lord shall be revealed, and all flesh shall see it together.' And he ended with his great cry for that day, 'when we allow freedom to ring – when we let it ring from every city and every hamlet, from every state and every city, we will be able to speed up that day when all of God's children, black men and white men, Jews and Gentiles, Protestants and Catholics, will be able to join hands and sing in the words of the old Negro spiritual, "Free at last, Free at last, Great God a-mighty, we are free at last". '

Prayer

Father in Heaven, grant us the joy of knowing that you came to set us free. May we sing for joy and thanksgiving this Advent and Christmas time when your Son came to visit us in great humility. Help us to be agents of love, hope and peace. Amen.

Reflection

Consider how we arise each day. What is the good news that we are expecting; what are our garments of glory? How can we be the light set on a hill that cannot be hidden?

WEEK 1: FRIDAY

Awaking into Life after Death (Revelation 21.1–4)

I saw a new heaven and a new earth, for the first heaven and the first earth had vanished, and there was no longer any sea. [2]I saw the Holy City, new Jerusalem, coming down out of heaven from God, made ready like a bride adorned for her husband. [3]I heard a loud voice proclaiming from the throne: 'Now God has his dwelling with humankind! He will dwell among them and they shall be his people, and God himself will be with them. [4]He will wipe every tear from their eyes. There shall be an end to death, and to mourning and crying and pain, for the old order has passed away!'

Here is a story of pain and darkness that our son Geoffrey, and his wife Beth, went through following the death of their child before she was born. As a father of a grieving son and daughter-in-law, all I could do was to stand with them, grieve with them, and pray that they would find that the words of Revelation 21 would, in time, be true in their lives.

This is the testimony Geoffrey wrote just seven weeks after the death of their daughter, Ruth. He spoke these words at Ruth's Funeral Service.

The Pain

What can a father say about a child he never got so see take her first breath? Never got to see take her first steps? Never got to see her cry out 'mummy' when she stubs her toe? Never got to see her eyes light up as she sees herself in her first princess dress? Never got to walk with her through her first disappointment? Never got to have her fall asleep in his arms? Never got to argue with her about that boy she has started spending a little too much time with? Never got to hear her say, 'Daddy, I love you ...'

Ruth's Legacy

Some would say that to get a true measure of someone's life you have to see how it affects the people they left behind. Well, our daughter has for ever changed us. Ruth you are loved so much by your mummy and daddy and you are an inspiration to us both.

This change, this sense of hope we feel, was not a foregone conclusion by any means. This transformation has astonished us and didn't seem at all likely seven weeks ago.

Hope Smashed

A few hours before Ruth's stillborn delivery, as I stood, with my parents, beside Beth in her hospital bed, I just started sobbing uncontrollably. It had hit me that God hadn't come through for us.

We thought she was going to be a miracle baby. We knew it would be against the odds, but we worship a God for whom nothing is impossible. But Ruth's heart had stopped beating. Our hope had died.

The previous Monday, at the 20-week scan, we found out that Ruth no longer had fluid surrounding her, and we'd been told that if she went full-term she wouldn't be able to breathe, and so we should consider terminating the pregnancy.

But a strange thing happened that week. Day by day our hope rose, as we spoke to experts and read testimonies of cases where the waters break early and the child goes on to live a long life. That chance was all we needed for our hope to rise again.

24

We knew that the pregnancy could end itself any time, but the heartbeat was strong, and though there was no fluid around the baby, what we could see was in perfect order. Plus we had God on our side. We had thought we were just staying a final night in hospital for observations before being discharged in the morning.

So, standing there sobbing at the end of the bed the next day, the fact that our hope had died hit me like a cannon ball to the heart. I just kept asking, 'Why?'

Why, God?

Why God, why? Why did you not act? Did you not hear our prayers? We thought you were good, but nothing about this is good.

So many times, during the pregnancy, we thought we had lost the baby, only for Ruth to defy the odds, and each time it felt God had come through for us. That our daughter was destined for this earth. So why would you keep coming through for her, and building our hope, only for her to be taken away like this?

But God Was Still There in the Midst

So many things just fell perfectly into place that let us know he was with us – from the amazing midwife who delivered Ruth, to friends and family being able to come and visit, meet her, and stand with us. The hugest gift was actually meeting Ruth.

Meeting Ruth

When I met Ruth, she was the most beautiful thing I'd ever seen. She was perfectly formed, about 10 inches in length, with her tiny little hands and feet. She even had all her little finger nails. She looked so peaceful, I just couldn't stop smiling.

Ruth is such a beautiful name, but I can't take credit for that – it was totally Beth's choice.

You probably know that her name is shared by a woman in the Bible, who had incredible faith despite going through so much grief and hardship. God wove a beautiful, redemptive tapestry in her life, and we're choosing to believe he's doing that for us too. Our tapestry isn't finished: it's a work in progress. If we're honest, it feels like a big jumble of threads right now, but we believe that one day we will see how beautiful it is, and we know that our Ruthie's beauty will be a huge part of that. Ruth is also my dad's mum's name, so that makes it extra special.

Saying Goodnight and Goodbye

We got to spend 24 hours with Ruth and we decided to say goodbye to her at the hospital by reading her the kids' book *Guess How Much I Love You.*

We lit a candle and read to her by candlelight, taking turns to read a page, whilst holding back the tears. Reading her the story was both the hardest and most beautiful moment of my life. We said our goodbyes, knowing that we wouldn't look on her face again in our lifetime.

I can definitely say that my daughter had enlarged my heart and increased my capacity to love. The way she fought so hard, and for so long, has inspired us not to give up. She has made me want to be a father even more.

It's Not Been Plain Sailing

The weeks following have been both tough and rewarding. There have been days when Beth just wants to stay in bed and cry, and times when I've tried to block it out by being busy. We've both had moments when we have felt it's not worth living anymore, that this pain is just too unbearable.

But since we met Ruth, we promised each other we would let ourselves feel whatever we feel, be open with each other and with God. We'd make a conscious effort to let him in, and we have found the easiest way to do that is by singing praises to him.

Singing praise in response reminds me of a God who came and died for me, that I may not only know him, but have eternal life, where I will get to play with my daughter, run through the fields with her, make her laugh, and see her totally free and filled with the Spirit of God.

The song 'So Will I' helped keep us steadfast during the pregnancy, and now it has taken on an added meaning for us both. The song reminds us that Christ died for Ruth, and we believe she is reaping that beautiful exchange in heaven right now.

> And as You speak
> A hundred billion failures disappear
> Where You lost Your life so I could find it here
> If You left the grave behind You so will I
> I can see Your heart in everything You've done
> Every part designed in a work of art called love
> If You gladly chose surrender so will I
> I can see Your heart
> Eight billion different ways
> Every precious one
> A child You died to save
> If You gave Your life to love them so will I
> Like You would again a hundred billion times
> But what measure could amount to Your desire
> You're the One who never leaves the one behind.

> (Joel Houston, Benjamin Hastings
> and Michael Fatkin)

Prayer

Father of life and love, help us to know your faithfulness in all things this Advent. In the pain and sorrow, as well as in the joy and hope of our lives, may we hold on to your promise of everlasting life. Amen.

Reflection

As we contemplate the loss of those we love, what are the promises from God which might give us hope? As we consider the reading from the Book of Revelation, and read the words of Geoffrey's reflection, what can we do or say to help those who are suffering this Advent?

WEEK 1: SATURDAY

Awaking to Glory (Isaiah 60.1-3, 19-22)

Arise, shine, Jerusalem, for your light has come; and over you the glory of the Lord has dawned. [2]Though darkness covers the earth and dark night the nations, on you the Lord shines and over you his glory will appear; [3]nations will journey towards your light and kings to your radiance. [19]The sun will no longer be your light by day, nor the moon shine on you by night; the Lord will be your everlasting light, your God will be your splendour. [20]Never again will your sun set nor your moon withdraw her light; but the Lord will be your everlasting light and your days of mourning will be ended. [21]Your people, all of them righteous, will possess the land forever. They are a shoot of my own planting, a work of my own hands for my adornment. [22]The few will become a

28

thousand; the handful, a great nation. At its appointed time
I the Lord shall bring this swiftly to pass.

'Wakey wakey, rise and shine', has long been the wake-up call for soldiers in the British Army: a trumpet call in the morning. It sounds like a modern version of Isaiah's call to the people of Israel, but the shining demanded of the British soldiers probably had more to do with paying attention to the state of their buttons and their boots than to the glory of the Lord.

As we said last Sunday, making the preparations for getting ready for the day can help our hearts and minds to be ready too. The soldiers who hear the wake-up call may be just as disinclined to tumble out of bed as we are when the alarm goes. But the training and discipline of their minds and bodies enables them to overcome their sluggishness, filling them with the energy and strength they need for the task.

We, as the army of the Lord, must always be ready to wake up, rise and shine with his reflected glory – as we are *being changed from Glory to Glory.*

Possibly we don't feel too sparkling first thing in the morning, but the brightness isn't our own, it is from the Lord; his glory has risen upon us and if we don't hide that glory we will be shining like the sun. The light of Christ is come into the world and it is to be seen so clearly etched on our faces and in our behaviour that all the world will turn to delight in its warming glow.

Tomorrow we will be lighting the second Advent Candle, the light is getting brighter, the coming of the Lord is closer. Traditionally the second Advent Candle helps us to remember the Prophets, and Isaiah is the Old

Testament prophet whose message is most closely linked to the coming of the Messiah. Once again we rejoice in his message of hope; the darkness of ignorance and sin is dissipated and we see things more clearly in the pure light from the One True Light.

Isaiah is warning of the deep, thick darkness of sin and unbelief which threatens to engulf the earth. In the desert days in Israel, Isaiah would have known what that deep darkness was like. Here in the UK it is hard to find a spot, even in the countryside, where darkness is complete. When you look at night pictures of the earth from space, the northern and western sections of the planet are a blaze of light.

I remember the darkness of rural places in Uganda, where I grew up – places that did not have sodium street lighting and electricity – and those of you who come from less inhabited places of the earth will know it too. In that deep, thick darkness that Isaiah describes, there can be a real sense of disorientation, a sapping of courage and spirit as we find no points of reference or direction. If we stay too long without light, a deep fear of loss can overcome us, a terror that light will not return. We should be even more afraid of the kind of spiritual darkness which Isaiah speaks about. The darkness which invades every part of our life – our mind, our heart, our soul, removing our compass, our sense of direction and our hope.

How much more glorious then is the promise of the glory of God coming upon us, the everlasting light of Jesus Christ dawning in our lives.

What is Isaiah's promise of light? That 'the Lord will be your everlasting light and your days of mourning will be ended. Your people, all of them righteous, will possess the land forever.'

Isaiah is bringing hope to the people of Israel in the Exile. Their years of mourning, their grief and sadness will come to an end. The people will be godly again, returned to his love and protection. They will no longer be stateless orphans.

This too is a promise for us. When the Christ, the Light of heaven and Sun of Righteousness came into the world, it was not only to liberate and restore the people of Israel, it was to liberate and restore the whole world to holiness and life. That is why this reading is often used in Epiphany: 'Nations shall come to your light, and kings to the brightness of your dawn.' And the wise men followed the light of the star, coming to celebrate the glorious birth of the Light to the world. With Christ's Great Commission, that light is taken to the ends of the earth. In these verses we are reminded of our call to make his light visible to all people – through our lives, and in our words and deeds.

Eighty years ago, in King George VI's 1939 Christmas broadcast, the King quoted Minnie Louise Haskins' poem:

> And I said to the man who stood at the gate of the year:
> 'Give me a light that I may tread safely into the
>   unknown.'
> And he replied:
> 'Go out into the darkness and put your hand into the
>   Hand of God.
> That shall be to you better than light and safer than a
>   known way.'
> So I went forth, and finding the Hand of God, trod
>   gladly into the night.
> And He led me towards the hills and the breaking of day
>   in the lone East.

Prayer

Lord, as we wake each morning may we put our hand into the hand of God, and welcome his glorious and life-giving light into our lives. Amen.

Reflection

Darkness can be a place where light has not found a way to enter.

Darkness can be a choice of behaviour, a turning away from the light.

If it is the darkness that *surrounds* us it may be our circumstances. It may be illness, poverty, oppression, hopelessness.

If it is the darkness *within us*, it may be lack of understanding, bitterness, unforgiveness or wilful sin.

Are there things in your life which are shutting out the light?

Isaiah gives us hope that light will come. Think about what you would like the light to do in your life.

WEEK 2: CLEAN UP!

Collect for the Second Sunday of Advent

O Lord, raise up, we pray, your power and come among us, and with great might succour us; that whereas, through our sins and wickedness we are grievously hindered in running the race that is set before us, your bountiful grace and mercy may speedily help and deliver us; through Jesus Christ your Son our Lord, to whom with you and the Holy Spirit, be honour and glory, now and for ever.

We begin our second week of Advent with a prayer that Christ's coming will help us and deliver us from our sins and wickedness – from the foolish self-destructive behaviour we indulge in if we remain as people of the darkness. We have a race to run, and we need to be fit and unencumbered in order to reach our goal.

I don't know if you've ever seen someone trying to run for a bus after a night's drinking. It's a painful sight. They can't keep in a straight line; they can't see clearly where they're going; their legs are weak and out of control. It's the same with someone carrying heavy unwieldy cases. The weight of the baggage takes them off-track, and slows them down.

Christ's grace and mercy set us free from the effects of our foolishness and enable us to run the race that is set before us – the long-distance journey into God, buoyed up by the power of the Holy Spirit, and the encouragement of the Cloud of Witnesses urging us on our way.

SECOND SUNDAY OF ADVENT

Clean Up for Action (Ephesians 5.11–20)

¹¹take no part in the barren deeds of darkness, but show them up for what they are. ¹²It would be shameful even to mention what is done in secret. ¹³But everything is shown up by being exposed to the light, and whatever is exposed to the light itself becomes light. ¹⁴That is why it is said: 'Awake, sleeper, rise from the dead, and Christ will shine upon you.' ¹⁵Take great care, then, how you behave: act sensibly, not like simpletons. ¹⁶Use the present opportunity to the full, for these are evil days. ¹⁷Do not be foolish, but understand what the will of the Lord is. ¹⁸Do not give way to drunkenness and the ruin that goes with it, but let the Holy Spirit fill you: ¹⁹speak to one another in psalms, hymns, and songs; sing and make music from your heart to the Lord; ²⁰and in the name of our Lord Jesus Christ give thanks every day for everything to our God and Father.

Our Bible reading from Ephesians continues last week's theme of waking up and, like today's Collect, takes us on to the next step – the need to *clean up our lives*. The Apostle Paul wants to make sure the Ephesian Christians avoid the kind of behaviour he condemns in the earlier verses of this chapter.

He therefore sets out the ways in which we can live as children of light:

1 Being light by avoiding the habits and behaviour of the dark.
2 Being light and exposing the things of darkness.
3 Being light by rejoicing in it and encouraging each other.

Unfortunately, waking up from sleep, particularly if the sleep has followed a night of intemperance, can be an uncomfortable experience. And if, in the clear light of day, the results of our foolishness are exposed to the view of others, it can be a shameful awakening.

Earlier this year the last ever edition of the *Yellow Pages Business Directory* was delivered. The older readers among you will remember some of the classic television advertisements for this publication. One of them showed a young man arriving home to find his flat door open. His neighbour, looking in at the chaos of his flat, sympathetically tells him, 'I'm afraid you've been burgled. They've completely ransacked the place.' Of course, the mess had been caused by the young man himself. His careless and self-indulgent lifestyle had wrecked his flat. But he only became truly aware of it when it was exposed to the view of others; only then was he able to see his life as others saw it. A life that had been invaded and wrecked.

'Take great care, then, how you behave', says the Apostle Paul. Take care of your life. It is precious. Don't let it be ruined by foolish behaviour. Don't let yesterday's folly rob you of today's possibilities.

It is probably true that more people run into danger – whether physical or spiritual – through thoughtlessness, carelessness or foolishness than through outright wickedness, and foolishness is a danger constantly warned against throughout the Bible, along with exhortations to seek wisdom. For example, the whole purpose of the Book of Proverbs is, as it says in Chapter 1, verses 2–3, 'by which mankind will come to wisdom and instruction, will understand words that bring understanding, ²and will attain to a well-instructed intelligence, righteousness, justice, and probity'. At the end of this introduction, the writer sums it up: 'The fear of the Lord is the foundation of knowledge; it is fools who scorn wisdom and instruction' (Proverbs 1.7). In each of the next thirty chapters, the dangers of foolishness are expounded.

Foolishness can be found in many areas of our life. Last week we saw the foolishness of being unaware, unprepared, lost in spiritual darkness and we looked at Advent alternatives to the foolish behaviour of the night.

Today, the Apostle Paul once again shows that there is also an alternative to foolish behaviour. Don't get drunk, but be filled with the Spirit. That feeling is better than drunkenness any day. Having a glass of wine is fine, but being drunk just takes you out of the joy of real life, as the build-up of alcohol slowly poisons your system. Being filled with the Spirit, on the other hand, gives you a greater sense of well-being, greater exhilaration, an even greater bubbling-over delight in the wonder of life. Singing drunken songs is not life-enhancing, but 'singing psalms and hymns and spiritual songs among yourselves' lifts your heart.

There have been scientific studies showing how singing can improve your health and well-being. One study I was reading recently lists a number of the physiological and emotional benefits:[1] it boosts your immune system; improves your strength and breathing capacity; improves your posture; helps with sleep; acts as an anti-depressant; lowers stress levels; and improves mental alertness. Singing with others widens your circle of friends; boosts your confidence; stimulates your brain; improves your

1 S. Clift and others, *Journal of Applied Arts and Health*, 2010.

communication skills and helps you appreciate other singers. All in all, 12 improvements in your life and health. How much more, then, might we expect the benefit to be if the *content* of the singing is also health-giving!

What is the Apostle Paul's alternative to foolish, unhealthy behaviour in the Ephesian Church? He says, '18Do not give way to drunkenness and the ruin that goes with it, but let the Holy Spirit fill you: 19speak to one another in psalms, hymns, and songs; sing and make music from your heart to the Lord; 20and in the name of our Lord Jesus Christ give thanks every day for everything to our God and Father' (Ephesians 5.18–20).

Last week we spoke about the wonderful music of Handel's *Messiah*. As the weeks of Advent go by, what better chance have we of hearing wonderful hymns and spiritual songs, wherever we go? At no other time of the year is there so much music on our airwaves – hymns and songs – whenever we go into shops, whenever we switch on the radio, the air is filled with joyful singing, celebrating the coming of Christmas. Even those people who may never sing any other kind of hymn will know the words of our beautiful songs of joy and love at this time of year.

For those of us singing Advent carols during this time, we can join in that sense of awe and waiting for the fulfilment of God's promise, and his gift to us.

Prayer

Lord Jesus, may our hearts be filled with thanksgiving, and our lips full of praise to you this Advent. May we unashamedly lift up our voices to welcome you. Amen.

Reflection

Consider the example of the power of solar panels, taking in the light and warmth of the sun, and using that energy to create light and warmth, and to pump water. The light of day provides light in the darkness and gives power to the fountain of life. Think of how the light and power of God drives our lives.

Look at two different kinds of conduit in your home – the central heating radiator, bringing heat and warmth, and the drainpipe draining water away. Ask yourself – 'What am I? A radiator or a drainpipe?'

WEEK 2: MONDAY

Clean Up to Find the Way (Matthew 7.13–16a)

[13]Enter by the narrow gate. Wide is the gate and broad the road that leads to destruction, and many enter that way; [14]narrow is the gate and constricted the road that leads to life, and those who find them are few. [15]Beware of false prophets, who come to you dressed up as sheep while underneath they are savage wolves. [16]You will recognize them by their fruit.

In Uganda, there is a Baganda saying that 'Anyone who has never travelled thinks that their mother is the best cook.' Travelling, especially on foot, opens our eyes to a new world full of adventure.

However, anyone who travels around any country by car can't go too far without coming across road construction work being carried out to create additional lanes to the motorway, or building bypasses to help speed u travelling. Local and national governments have budgets set aside for road widening schemes, and this policy is usually very popular with the travelling public, once the disruption of roadworks is over. A wide road is thought of as being a good road; it gets us to our destination quickly, unlike some of the narrow one-horse lanes we have to travel on when we get off the motorway, where it can be frustrating to get stuck behind slow traffic with no chance of overtaking.

Yet Jesus says something counter-intuitive – enter by the narrow gate, go along the narrow way, that's definitely the way to travel. Of course it may be difficult to convince all those speeding to their destination along the motorway, with the countryside just a blur – choosing a narrow winding slow route just isn't an option when life is so pressing and speed is of the essence.

Yet Jesus says there are only two ways to travel: one way is narrow and difficult, but it leads to life; the other is wide and seems easy, but leads to destruction.

This is a message which hasn't changed through all the ages of God's story with humankind.

Psalm 1 sets it out clearly. Blessed are they who follow the way of the Lord, who delight in his law rather than the way of sinners, for 'the LORD watches over the way of the righteous, but the way of the wicked is doomed,' says the psalmist.

Jesus is telling his disciples the same truth, and he explains it further by affirming that he alone is The Way, the way of righteousness, the way to everlasting life.

The message is the same for us today. There are only two ways to live our life: Our own way or His way.

There is a song made popular by Frank Sinatra, which

is often chosen for funerals, 'My Way'. I often wonder if people are really aware of the implications of the lyrics of this song, particularly in the last verse. The man who wants to do it his way is someone taking pride in trusting only in himself; whose words are not 'the words of one who kneels', but the words of one who did it his own way. The words of someone who believes he owns the way.

We need to think about who does own the ways. There is a clue – one leads to life, the other leads to death. And the character of the owner is also visible in the two ways.

On the wide way, we see people caught up in selfish, aimless pursuits, the kind of behaviour the Apostle Paul was warning about when he called people to wake up from the darkness of their lives and embrace the light.

Yet those who are walking the narrow way, have Jesus Christ at the centre of their living, thinking, goal and rejoicing – such people bear fruit in all its fullness: life in the Holy Spirit.

Little by little as we walk that narrow way, grace, kindness, tenderness grow in us.

'I am the gate', Jesus tells his listeners in John 10.7 (NRSV) – the gateway to our safe haven, and to all that is lovely and wholesome for our growth. He does not shut the door to anyone who comes to him; they may enter and move about freely, but they must pass through him, to know him and be known by him.

The disciples in Jesus Christ's time would be familiar with both the image of the gate to the sheepfold, and also the image of the narrow way. In ancient walled cities like Jerusalem there were many gates through the walls. Some were wide, where merchants could come with their goods, or where larger numbers of people could pass easily.

Others were small and narrow and these unobtrusive gates in a city wall were quite often the only safe way in and out, particularly if the city was under siege.

The walls of the city of York – like many other ancient walled cities – also contain these small safe gates. In York and some of the older towns in the UK, there are numerous small alleyways. These are called 'snickets' in York and 'ginnels' elsewhere. Along these narrow ways, one person may walk, or possibly two, but no more with comfort. There is no room to carry much baggage if you're using them. You need to travel light. Jesus referred to such a narrow way when he told his listeners that, 'It is easier for a camel to pass through the eye of a needle than for a rich man to enter the kingdom of God' (Mark 10.25). If we embark on a narrow way, we need to travel lightly. But the good thing about travelling the narrow way is that it's difficult to get lost – you can't wander from the pathway, because it is Jesus Christ. He is *the Way*, we must walk him. Because Jesus Christ is *the Truth*, we must know him. Because Jesus Christ is *Life*, we must live him.

You can't always see the end of the path when you start down the narrow way. It can sometimes seem hard and lonely, and you need faith to step into it. Yet we have a purpose as we go forward – to reach the light – and then restraint and obedience becomes a delight. There may be many on the wide way that you can see and join with, and on a narrow way there may be many, but you don't always see them. They may have gone ahead of you; they may be following behind. But on the narrow way, Christ will accompany you, even when you feel alone.

At the beginning of our lives, we all start out on the broad path, and we stay on that way until we hear Jesus Christ's voice leading us into the narrow way. Your parents or friends may direct you to the narrow way but, in the end, you have to make the decision.

Our task is to commend the narrow way, to take others to Jesus, the Way, so that they can find that small gate, that small alleyway amidst all the wider more obvious ways.

Prayer

Heavenly Father, may we always look for the Narrow Way, Jesus Christ, who leads to the true light. May we follow him without distraction, and draw others to the fire of his love. Amen.

Reflection

Is our task this Advent to discover what is the Narrow Way to follow? Consider what the signposts are for the wide road and the narrow way. What signs should we be on the alert for?

WEEK 2: TUESDAY

Clean Up from the Inside Out (Mark 7.20–23)

[20]He went on, 'It is what comes out of a person that defiles him. [21]From inside, from the human heart, come evil thoughts, acts of fornication, theft, murder, [22]adultery, greed, and malice; fraud, indecency, envy, slander, arrogance, and

folly; ²³all these evil things come from within, and they are what defile a person.'

Many, many years ago, I saw the wonderful musical *Fiddler on the Roof,* which has recently had another London revival. The main character, Tevye, is the father of three daughters and, as their tradition demands, seeks help from the Matchmaker in finding suitable husbands for them. However, he is forced to confront his attitudes to tradition when one by one his daughters seek to marry someone of their own choice. Times are changing. His first instinct when faced with challenges to the traditions of their community is to exclaim, 'Unheard of, absurd … Unthinkable … '

The religious elite in Jerusalem were similarly strident in their reaction to the behaviour of Jesus and his disciples. Jesus hadn't required them to wash in the traditional way before eating! 'Unheard of! Unthinkable!' Without washing in that particular way, they were defiling themselves: making themselves unclean!

What arrogance to tell the One who alone was clean that he had defiled himself! The Pharisees' position was always to try to claim the moral high ground – standing firm on the importance of tradition and law. But Jesus saw through their play-acting. Jesus said, 'How right Isaiah was when he prophesied about you hypocrites in these words: "This people pays me lip-service, but their heart is far from me: they worship me in vain, for they teach as doctrines the commandments of men." You neglect the commandment of God, in order to maintain the tradition of men' (Mark 7.6–8).

He continues, 'Let's look at the way you behave; how you

bend your own laws and traditions, using the tradition of "Corban" – setting aside money for God – to avoid helping your parents' (Mark 7.9–13).

This is how we might hear it today:

> Well mother, I know you are feeling the cold a bit, but actually when you think about it, you're in a fortunate position – you have somewhere to live and plenty of warm clothes. Of course I would help you if I could, but I'm committed to double tithing at church and what little I have after that is set aside for charities. We here in the west are very fortunate – we have the welfare state, you have a pension and supplementary benefits; after all, that's what we pay our taxes for. I'm sure you'd agree with me that my priority should be to help those who are in far greater need than we are.

So what *is* unclean?

Jesus explained that *what* goes in and out of a person in the way of food – and *how* it goes in and out – isn't the issue. This would certainly make his listeners wake up. This is a radical down-to-earth way of looking at the 'dos' and 'don'ts' that would take a lot of getting used to. It wasn't a lesson they learned easily. In fact, it wasn't until much later that Peter finally learned the lesson, when God gave him a vision of animals of every kind, including those that were regarded profane or unclean, and invited him three times to 'get up, kill and eat' (Acts 10.10–16). Only then did Peter see that God was showing him that he must not call anyone profane or unclean (Acts 10.28).

It's what lives in a person's heart – where his allegiance is, what his motives are, whose authority he's under –

that's what makes someone unclean or profane. If there is corruption in the heart it will lead to corrupt behaviour. And you can't paper over the cracks by keeping traditions and laws which make you look as though you're still pure. It's not about whether you can pull the wool over your neighbours' eyes and make them think you're perfect; it's about whether you're acting as part of God's kingdom of love, justice and peace, or as part of the enemy's.

Keeping external rules won't change the heart. There can only be in-depth cleansing of the heart through rebirth by the Holy Spirit.

The trouble with living by rules and traditions is that we end up believing our own propaganda. Because the rules are man-made, there is no end to our 'improving on them', as the Pharisees and Scribes did in the time of Jesus of Nazareth. Simple washing for hygiene becomes complicated ritualistic washing for show. Putting on a show means that we end up deceiving ourselves, and then others. It's the drip, drip, drip of self-deception day-by-day – maybe just about little things – that can harden our hearts and stop us from seeing the truth.

In a town called Knaresborough, not far from York, there is a famous cave in the limestone rock of that area. Water runs down the wall of the cave and drips down very slowly turning things below it into stone. Over the years, visitors have hung objects on the wall to catch the drips – hats, bags and lots of teddy bears – which are now like stone ornaments hanging over the entrance to the cave. The story goes that it takes about two months to turn a little teddy to stone.

I wonder how long it takes to turn our human heart to stone? And can we reverse the process?

What comes out of the heart shows what we are, or what we desire, or what we aspire to, Jesus tells his disciples. No amount of washing will change that.

Lady Macbeth knew this well. Following the murder of the king, her conscience and her sleep are disturbed, as her mind continues to see the blood on her hands, however hard she scrubs them, 'Out, damned spot! Out, I say! – One, two. Why, then, 'tis time to do't … What will these hands ne'er be clean?' (*Macbeth* 5:1)

How can we be clean – be born again by water and the Holy Spirit, find the real us, the real new cleansed us? Only by being washed clean by Jesus. Not by 'holy water' alone, or water from special places. Not by washing at certain times or in certain ways. Cleanliness isn't achieved through works, but by simple obedience to the God who, in Jesus Christ, makes all things new. As St Paul says, 'Anyone united to Christ: New Creation' (2 Corinthians 5.17a).

Jesus wasn't just holding the religious leaders up for scorn – he was warning us all. He came to expose the hearts of everyone, and to help us see what is hiding in the dark corners of our lives. Hypocrisy (play-acting) has many ways of sneaking up on us, and hypocrisy is a tool that the enemy of our souls is expert at using against us, and against truth.

C. S. Lewis's *Screwtape Letters* takes the form of a series of letters from a senior demon, Screwtape, to his nephew, Wormwood, a Junior Tempter, in his attempts to secure the damnation of a man Screwtape refers to as 'The Patient'. An important piece of advice to Wormwood is,

Keep his mind off the most elementary duties by directing it to the most advanced and spiritual ones.

Aggravate that most useful human characteristic, the horror and neglect of the obvious. You must bring him to a condition in which he can practise self-examination for an hour without discovering any of those facts about himself, which are perfectly clear to anyone who has ever lived in the same house with him or worked the same office.

This Advent, let us heed Jesus Christ's warning against spiritual complacency, and blindness to the dangers which threaten our purity of heart. Are we awake to the dangers of being a 'Patient' for a modern-day Wormwood, distracting us into thinking *Our Way* outweighs *Christ's Way*, or convincing us that an outward show is enough? Are our hearts ready to be renewed and cleansed by Jesus Christ's loving action?

As we journey through Advent, as we learn to wake up and stay alert, as we were remembering last week, may we also *Clean Up* by letting Jesus Christ renew our hearts so that everything that comes out of us shows his love and beauty.

Prayer

Lord Jesus Christ, help us to come again to you every day, and ask to be made clean so that our lives display the fruits of the Spirit and the love and hope you bring to us all. Amen.

Reflection

Things don't change very much. People still argue with Jesus – sometimes because they don't like some of his ideas, sometimes because they have a particular tradition they're hanging on to.

Think about how you regard tradition. Jaroslav Pelikan, in *The Vindication of Tradition* (1983 Jefferson Lecture in the Humanities), said, 'Tradition is the living faith of the dead, traditionalism is the dead faith of the living. And, I suppose I should add, it is traditionalism that gives tradition such a bad name.'[2]

Metropolitan Anthony (Bloom) of Sourozh, referring to Pelikan's statement, responded, 'Tradition is the living memory of almost two thousand years of Christianity, living and kept alive by the action and the inspiration of the Holy Spirit and made solid, unshakeable by the word and the person of Christ.'[3]

Consider where you have seen that *traditionalism* begins to outweigh *truth*, or when '*Our way*' begins to outweigh '*His way*'.

WEEK 2: WEDNESDAY

Clean Up Wholeheartedly (Joel 2.12–13)

[12]Yet even now, says the Lord, turn back to me wholeheartedly with fasting, weeping, and mourning. [13]Rend your hearts and not your garments, and turn back to the LORD your God, for he is gracious and compassionate, long-suffering and ever constant, ready always to relent when he threatens disaster.

---

2 Jaroslav Pelikan, *The Vindication of Tradition*: 1983 Jefferson Lecture in the Humanities (1984), p. 65.

3 http://www.russianpresence.org.uk/index.php/history/3060-anthony-of- sourozh.html

We are in the season of pantomime. Whether it's *Goose, Cinderella* or *Jack and the Beanstalk*, we all the form: our heroes are a poor girl or boy, downtrodden by the baddies' greed or double-dealing (boo!); but they are rescued and restored by a fairy godmother or Prince Charming (hooray!). We know it's all make-believe, and we go through the various rituals – 'Oh, no he isn't, Oh, yes he is' – with great gusto, knowing all will be well in the end.

Pantomime is fun, but there are situations when play-acting just isn't going to work. That's when real badness is destroying lives, and real rescue requires more than a fairy godmother waving a wand.

Yesterday we were reading about the play-acting hypocrisy of some of the religious leaders who called into question Jesus Christ's leadership, and tried to throw doubt on his 'soundness' by challenging his adherence to religious tradition.

Jesus pointed out the need for true purity of heart which could only come from responding to God's cleansing.

The religious teachers should not have been surprised, for this was not a new teaching. Nearly nine centuries earlier, the Prophet Joel had called on the people of God to demonstrate integrity in their repentance. The ceremonial tearing of garments to show grief or penitence had become an empty ritual. Sometimes it is an exaggerated 'pantomime' of grief or simulated virtue.

Before Prophet Joel's call to repentance, the people of Israel may have thought they had some cause to relax and enjoy life a little. They had returned from exile, the temple had been rebuilt, they had been restored to where they felt they belonged, and they might have felt that all should be well with the world. Then came a plague of locusts – swarming over their beloved land and eating everything down to the roots, rather like the pitiless invading armies some of the older generation in Jerusalem might have remembered. What was going on! Why had God restored them only to devastate them again? The people had become complacent; in their restored comfort they had begun to forget the Lord, and think that merely acting out piety was sufficient.

Here in the UK, of course, we don't have experience of locust swarms. We may suffer from the depredations of slugs or squirrels in our gardens, and in the past our farmers have been affected by BSE decimating our cattle or other diseases attacking our sheep or pig farming. Yet in some African countries, and formerly in the Middle East, locust swarms have brought devastation on a huge scale. Tens of millions of insects can move through crops in minutes stripping them bare and leaving a wasteland where the people face famine and years of want. The people of Israel certainly had cause to mourn in the face of that destruction of their livelihood and their hopes. What could they do? What could God do, now?

Prophet Joel calls for the people to offer wholehearted repentance, with hearts turning to God for cleansing and complete renewal, and later, in verse 25, God assures the repentant people that he would compensate them for the years the locusts had eaten – the 'locust years' of hardship and suffering.

What do we know of locust years? Here in the UK, in the second week of Advent, we are surrounded by lovely Christmas decorations brightening our streets and our houses. Here on our 42-inch television screens we see advertisements for all the delights that can be bought and enjoyed as we revel in this season of pleasure and magic.

Yet on those same television screens, between the advertisements, we may see news of poverty, people-trafficking, violence, anger, famine across the world. How

sickness in the family; broken and suffering nearer to home: and anxiety about money. The misery ~~~nships; depression where the locust years are present and damaging.

For all these situations, as for the people of Israel in the time of the Prophet Joel, God promises that he will restore to us the years the locusts have taken if we return to him 'wholeheartedly with fasting, weeping and mourning.'

[8]If we claim to be sinless, we are self-deceived and the truth is not in us. [9]If we confess our sins, he is just and may be trusted to forgive our sins and cleanse us from every kind of wrongdoing. [10]If we say we have committed no sin; we make him out to be a liar and his word has no place in us.

(1 John 1.8–9)

Proverbs (28.13) says, 'Conceal your offences, and you will not prosper; confess and renounce them, and you will obtain mercy.'

In this second week of Advent as we approach the ~~come.~~ Jesus reconciled us through his death and resurrection and that is fantabulous. Yet we look around and see the locusts and the devastation. There is so much more reconciliation to be achieved. God longs for us with compassion and friendliness.

Two years ago, around this time a young friend of mine called Ellie was waiting to have open heart surgery to replace a valve which had been damaged by severe infection ten years earlier. During that time of sickness, she was on life-support in hospital for several weeks, and I was in the habit of dropping in after evening meetings to pray over her unconscious form. After septicaemia's damage and one day the doctors warned her parents that they could do no more – only wait and hope. I called in to pray later than usual that evening, and as I sat and prayed by Ellie's bed, I was confronted by a nurse I hadn't seen before. She aggressively asked for my ID and demanded that I leave the ward immediately. I explained that I knew Ellie and that I was a frequent visitor, but she insisted, loudly, that I leave. Amazingly, her shouting seemed to rouse Ellie from her coma, and she opened her eyes and said angrily, 'I know him. He's my mum's boss.' She had awoken. And from that time she began to recover. But during the next ten years, the damage done to her heart meant that she suffered from increasing exhaustion and struggled to do her work or look after her family with the energy she would have liked. In the new year of 2018, by the grace of God and the skill of surgeons, her heart was repaired and renewed. The locust years are now being repaid and she gives thanks that God is a God of renewal.

I think of another woman, Carrie, who was being cared for by her sister as I walked on the Scalby Road in the pouring rain, on a very cold Sunday afternoon, on 30 January 2016, during my six-months' pilgrimage. She had suffered from chronic fatigue syndrome for twenty years, from the moment her father died. By the roadside, as I prayed for her, a dark cloud was lifted. A month later she wrote to me to say that 'You helped me to know that I am not alone. Jesus is now beside me, helping me and I am learning to listen to him.'

'Return to me wholeheartedly', God tells his people – with a whole heart, with nothing held back, with no pretence, no play-acting.

What does that mean for us this Advent? How can we return to God and be whole-hearted in everything we are doing?

Returning to God means that we need to be aware of Christ's presence in all things. Emmanuel – God with us is what we are celebrating. And we can celebrate our awareness of his presence in all things – as we cook; as we join with friends to make merry; as we sing carols; as we rush around the shops buying food and gifts. God is with us, and our hearts must return to him each day to repent of our forgetfulness, and acknowledge that he is Lord of all we do. I loved the motto in my mother's kitchen: 'Divine Service Offered Here Three Times A Day'. Yes, he is Lord in the kitchen, too!

Prayer (from a beautiful Motet by Thomas Tallis: 'Purge me O Lord')

'Purge me, O Lord, from all my sin and save thou me by
    faith from ill,
that I may rest and dwell with thee upon thy holy blessed
    hill
and that done, grant that with true heart I may without
    hypocrisy
affirm the truth, detract no man, but do all things with
    equity'. Amen.

Reflection

God needs more than our traditions, our forms of worship; he needs whole-hearted worship, witness, prayer and service from clean hearts.

Are you living through the 'locust years'? In what ways can you turn to God for his comfort and restoration?

WEEK 2: THURSDAY

Clean Up to Join the Celebration (Matthew 22.11–14)

[11]"When the king came in to watch them feasting, he observed a man who was not dressed for a wedding. [12]"My friend," said the king, "how do you come to be here without wedding clothes?" But he had nothing to say. [13]The king then said to his attendants, "Bind him hand and foot; fling him out into the dark, the place of wailing and grinding of teeth." [14]For many are invited, but few are chosen.'

The party season is upon us. Office parties, children's parties, church parties, formal and informal. Even some wedding parties, as Christmas weddings have become more popular. Does this fill you with delighted anticipation or dismay?

People's responses to party invitations are very varied. Someone I know always answers any invitation, however formal, by saying, 'I'll only come if I don't have to dress up'. But it's not just about us. As a bishop and archbishop, I've been privileged to attend some of the Queen's garden parties. They are special occasions to which a diverse group of people are invited in honour of their work and service to the country. There is a dress code – morning dress, uniform or traditional dress – and people conform to this out of respect for the Queen and for one another. Someone insisting on turning up in their usual jeans and trainers would soon be shown the door.

Yet Jesus's story isn't quite like this. If you read Chapter 22 from the beginning, you will see that what we have here is another wedding story, another parable where the Kingdom of God is likened to a wedding banquet.

The story actually comes a few chapters before the story of the unprepared scatter-brained bridesmaids in Chapter 25 of Matthew's Gospel. This time we have a story about the wedding guests. The preparations have all been made. Many gracious invitations had been sent out to the king's beloved guests. Enough food for a huge gathering has been cooked and temptingly displayed – but the invited guests did not turn up! They made lame excuses which were almost as insulting as an outright refusal. Have you ever gone to the trouble of inviting people for dinner only to have them tell you, at the last minute, that that's the night their favourite sit-com or soap opera, that has been running for years, is on. It is their 'reality therapy' and they can't miss the next episode. Or, like George Bernard Shaw's response to a high society 'At Home' invitation, when he replied, 'George Bernard Shaw: Also At Home!'

The king in Jesus Christ's parable was outraged, but his generosity was not to be wasted. His servants were sent with the instruction to give an invitation to everyone they could find in the city streets, or in the highways and byways, and soon the banquet hall was full of happy guests.

Yet then, as we read in today's verses, the king sees

someone not wearing a wedding robe. The result – the inappropriately dressed guest is thrown into the outer darkness.

This seems a very unexpected and disturbing reaction from the one who had so graciously reached out with his invitation to all and sundry. It seems to present an aspect of the king's character that we find rather lacking in serenity, given the fact that his instruction to his servants at the last minute was to go and find anyone they could find in the city streets, highways and byways, to fill his banqueting hall.

So how are we to understand this stern action of the king in this parable? Is it contradictory?

First, we can see in the story that the king is generous:

1 He is generous to his chosen guests, his friends and family – graciously inviting them to share his joy in the wedding banquet. When they refuse …

2 He is generous to the next group who are invited. Everyone who can be found, regardless of status or standing, is welcome to share in the banquet. The first group of invitees were found unworthy, because they rejected his call. The second group are found worthy by virtue of his invitation and their acceptance of it.

And what of the guests?

1 Neither group of guests had done anything to deserve the king's invitation. It was offered to them only through his grace and loving kindness.

2 The first group of invited guests did not show up – they decided they had better things to do. Their lives were all that mattered to them and the invitation of

the king was not a priority. The phrase 'not turning up' has a particular resonance with football fans. If their team plays poorly and doesn't try, it is often said of them, 'They may be a good team, but they didn't turn up today'. They may have been on the pitch, but they weren't really giving anything of themselves. The example of the guests who didn't show up should make us look at our own lives and consider what we are actually doing in response to what God has offered us in Jesus Christ.

3 The second group of guests may not have expected to be invited, but they responded and made the decision to be there.

So what are we to make of the *guest without the wedding garment*? Does it seem unfair to us that someone gathered up in a general invitation to everyone in the streets should then be condemned because of his inappropriate clothes?

Let's remember what we were thinking about at the beginning of last week when we were contemplating our actions on waking from the darkness. The Apostle Paul exhorted his friends in Rome and Thessalonica to clothe themselves in the Lord Jesus Christ. When we enter the Banquet of the King, he will be able to see whether or not we have put on the Lord Jesus Christ. That is the only appropriate dress for entering the Kingdom. The one who can tell the sheep from the goats, who sees whether we have lived lives of love and justice, friendliness and generosity, or whether we have lived lives of uncaring self-indulgence, can tell whether we are properly dressed for the great wedding feast when Christ comes again.

As our reading shows, some people have always wanted to respond to God by dictating their own terms. Will we reject his gracious and generous invitation to be citizens of his Kingdom, here and now, and yet still come? Will we give only a grudging acceptance, but insist we do it 'Our Way'? As he comes to us, holding out his hand in loving invitation, will we be ready to join unconditionally and wholeheartedly in God's great party? The man who was 'not dressed for a wedding', though pulled in from the street, did not go home to change into appropriate clothes he might have had. This was a royal wedding: a very big event! Yes, the invitation was free, but with freedom comes responsibility. When challenged by the king, why was he 'speechless'? What made him dress inappropriately? Dressing appropriately, in this parable of Jesus of Nazareth, reminds me of four graduation experiences – once at Makere and three times at Cambridge – wearing graduation robes. It certainly increased my sharpness and awareness that the graduation ceremony was important. Similarly, when I was ordained deacon, priest and bishop, I learned how vital it is to prepare myself in every way, including dress, as a way of honouring others and the task ahead.

The phrase 'fling him out into the dark, the place of wailing and grinding of teeth' has often been regarded in Christian tradition as referring to hell. If it does, how should we read it here? St Isaac the Syrian, I think, comes to the nub of the question that has bothered a lot of readers concerning hell. He says, 'Those who are tormented in hell are tormented by the invasion of love. What is there more bitter and violent than the pains of love? Those who feel they have sinned against love bear in themselves a damnation much heavier than the most dreaded punishments. The suffering with which sinning against love afflicts the heart is more keenly felt than any other torment. It is absurd to assume that the sinners in hell are deprived of God's love. Love is offered impartially, but by its very power it acts in two ways. It torments sinners, as happens here on earth when we are tormented by the presence of a friend to whom we have been unfaithful; and it gives joy to those who have been faithful. That is what the torment of hell is in my opinion: remorse. Yet love inebriates the souls of the sons and daughters of heaven by its delectability.'[4]

This comes very close to the parable of the rich man and Lazarus in Luke (16.23–25), where torment isn't just physical pain but looks very much like the spiritual torture of remorse.

Prayer

Heavenly Father, may we be ready and willing to respond to your gracious invitation when you call us. May we each day put on Jesus Christ, so that we are clothed in those beautiful wedding garments and ready to turn up whenever you come again. Amen.

Reflection

Our Father's Christmas Gift to us is the free gift of eternal life. But are we ready to receive it? Are we cleaned up and receptive or do we put off getting rid of our bad habits, our addictions, our selfish attitudes?

---

4 https://solzemli.wordpress.com/2011/02/24/saint-isaac-the-syrian-on-hell/. See also *The Spiritual Word of Isaac the Syrian* by Hilarion Alfeyev (Cistercian Publications, 2000), p. 280.

Are we clothed and ready to join the King's great banquet?

What remains for us to do to be ready, in this time of waiting?

WEEK 2: FRIDAY

Clean Up to Serve (Mark 1.29–31)

²⁹On leaving the synagogue they went straight to the house of Simon and Andrew; and James and John went with them. ³⁰Simon's mother-in-law was in bed with a fever. As soon as they told him about her, ³¹Jesus went and took hold of her hand, and raised her to her feet. The fever left her, and she attended to their needs.

I wonder if those of you who qualify have had your flu jab yet? I hope you have. At this time of year, just when we are at our busiest, we are often beset by colds and flu, fevers which lay us low and take all our energy. We lie in bed, unable to move or eat, aching in every part of our body, with our head swimming, our throat burning. This is how Jesus and Peter found Peter's mother-in-law when they returned from the synagogue one Sabbath.

If your mother was lying in bed with a high fever, I wonder what your reaction would be if your spouse brought home four guests for lunch after church!

This little story happens right at the start of Jesus Christ's ministry. In the first 28 verses of Mark's Gospel we hear, in swift succession, about Jesus Christ's baptism by John the Baptist, his temptation in the wilderness, his calling of the disciples, and his healing of a man with an unclean spirit in the synagogue. The Apostle Luke, in Chapter 4, also tells this story and gives additional detail of Jesus teaching in the synagogue, where he announced the beginning of his ministry by reading the words of Isaiah (61.1–2), 'The Spirit of the Lord God is upon me, because the Lord has anointed me; he has sent me to announce good news to the humble, to bind up the broken-hearted, to proclaim liberty to captives, release to those in prison; to proclaim a year of the Lord's favour.'

He goes on, as he does in the Gospel of Mark, to heal the man with the unclean spirit.

Jesus clearly chooses to suit the action to the word. He is ready to demonstrate what he later affirms, that, 'The sabbath was made for humankind, and not humankind for the sabbath' (Mark 2.27 NRSV).

In fulfilling the words of Isaiah's prophesy, he is not bound by traditions which hamper God's gracious plan for our health and well-being.

Isaiah (53.4) also prophesied about the Messiah's healing ministry: in Chapter 53 verse 4, he says, 'Yet it was our affliction he was bearing, our pain he endured, while we thought him smitten by God, struck down by disease and misery'. From the very start, Jesus of Nazareth's ministry is to cleanse and heal.

Why do people fall sick? Why was Peter's mother-in-law sick?

As we read the Gospels, it becomes clear that sickness, disability, mental health problems are regarded by the people of those times as stemming from sin. These days, our doctors are very unlikely to diagnose sin as a cause of illness! Though some illness may be considered to be caused by our own or others' careless living, we also know that sickness is a condition which can attack the righteous and the unrighteous alike.

Yet there is some sense in which the disobedience of Adam brought about sickness. The coming of the Son of God in our human flesh was in order to deal with that disobedience, to confront and overcome evil and the world's idolatry.

Sin came into the world with the turning away of the first Adam from the love of God. The deliberate disobedience and self-centred choices of the first members of the human race brought death into the world. Jesus came to bring light and life, to cleanse and restore us to the way we were created, to fit us for a return to Life, just as it says in the refrain of the lovely Westlife song, 'You Raise Me Up'. This picture of being raised up is a refrain throughout Jesus Christ's ministry.

In this early healing, we read, 'Jesus went and took hold of her hand, and raised her to her feet. The fever left her, and she attended to their needs.'

We read later that Jesus took the hand of Jairus's daughter and raised her up, and she returned to life; he raised the Widow of Nain's son from death; he called Lazarus up from the tomb, and he himself rose from the dead. All these images of sickness and death are given light and hope as Jesus enters the story, and calls the suffering person to rise up.

During my Pilgrimage of Prayer, Witness and Blessing, a mother and father (Jean and Peter Waller) invited me to visit their daughter, Susan Hazelwood, who was lying in the 'End of Life' bed in St Catherine's Hospice in Scarborough and she was not expected to survive the afternoon. She was slipping away fast. Susan had not spoken much for several days. I started praying the Lord's Prayer. Half-way through, Susan opened her eyes and joined in, and then thanked me for coming. Her whole face became radiant and there was peace and serenity all around her. Susan, a beloved lover of Jesus Christ, died thirteen days later. Her parents said, 'Visiting Susan at the end of her life was very hard. Your visit and prayers helped us a great deal and Susan found peace with God and her family. Thank you.'

Another God incident happened on 6 April 2011 at 3.30 p.m. I visited the Oscar Romero Project based in St Helen's Church Athersley, and also the vicarage where I met the vicar's wife, Marilyn Marshall.

She was clearly dying. I prayed for her and laid on her head my El Salvadorian Pectoral Cross (made for me by an orphan with the inscription on the back words of Archbishop Oscar Romero: 'Peace will flower when love and justice pervade our environment'). I then anointed her with the oil of gladness. To everyone's surprise, including her GP who was present at the time, she was restored to fullness of life. She went back to her job in a school, and when I visited to bless the new school, she was there to celebrate, along with her GP who exclaimed that he had never seen anything like her recovery. She told her story in my *Hope Stories* book.[5] Sadly, Marilyn died in 2016, and her husband, Rodney, died in 2018.

As I said at the beginning, I hope that those of you who can have had your flu jab – and indeed your pneumonia jab too. Vaccines are a wonderful invention and have the possibility of saving us from a lot of infection and discomfort, if not worse. However useful vaccinations

---

5 John Sentamu, *Hope Stories* (Darton Longman Todd: London, 2014), Ch. 20.

are, they can't stop everything. In December 1990 I had a very severe bout of pneumonia and spent six weeks in King's College Hospital, and more recently, I have gone down with flu, even after having been vaccinated. When I raised this with the doctor, he explained that there are so many varieties of virus that the makers of the vaccine can't anticipate them all. Infections can come, even when we think we are protected.

Similarly, in our day-to-day lives we may feel we're getting along very well and we are quite disconcerted if something lays us or our Christian friends low. Surely, if we go to church, read the Bible, say our prayers, we should be safe from being laid low by family breakdown, mental health issues, loneliness and all the other troubles and pressures of life. Surely we shouldn't find ourselves feeling weak and helpless in the face of situations we can't deal with, our heads spinning when faced with decisions we can't make, our bodies and wills feeble and powerless to act the way we know we should? The Apostle Paul understood that these fevers and pains, the pressures of life, sometimes even our own choices, can lay us low. He expressed this in his letter to the Romans when he said, '[14]We know that the law is spiritual; but I am not: I am unspiritual, sold as a slave to sin. [15]I do not even acknowledge my own actions as mine, for what I do is not what I want to do, but what I detest. [16]But if what I do is against my will, then clearly I agree with the law and hold it to be admirable. [17]This means that it is no longer I who perform the action, but sin that dwells in me. [18]For I know that nothing good dwells in me – my unspiritual self, I mean – for though the will to do good is there, the ability to effect it is not. [19]The good which I want to do, I fail to do; but what I do is the wrong which is against my will; [20]and if what I do is against my will, clearly it is no longer I who am the agent, but sin that has its dwelling in me' (Romans 7.14–20).

Jesus Christ has come to revitalize us and restore us. The fever and pressures of life may knock us down, but Jesus takes our hand and raises us up again. What was the response of Peter's mother-in-law when Jesus lifted her out of her sickness? She immediately began to serve them. She was given back her sense of purpose and her natural disposition – to be hospitable and welcoming. We too, when Jesus Christ raises us up from incapacity of any kind, turn to him in love and service, offering our lives for his purposes.

Prayer

Lord Jesus,
May we turn to you each day to heal and cleanse us from the fevers of life that lay us low, and sap our will to love and serve you and one another. Raise us up each day to health and strength to live for you. Amen.

Reflection

What are the things in your life – particularly at this time of year – that sap your energy, or lay you low? What changes can you make in your life in order to receive the strength to do the good things you want to do, and shake off the debilitating effects of wrong choices?

WEEK 2: SATURDAY

Clean Up for Life

O Breath of life, come sweeping through us,
Revive Thy church with life and power;
O Breath of life come, cleanse, renew us,
And fit Thy church to meet this hour.

O Wind of God, come bend us, break us,
Till humbly we confess our need;
Then in Thy tenderness remake us,
Revive, restore; for this we plead.

O Breath of love, come breathe within us,
Renewing thought and will and heart;
Come, Love of Christ, afresh to win us,
Revive Thy church in ev'ry part.

Revive us Lord! Is zeal abating
While harvest fields are vast and white?
Revive us, Lord, the world is waiting,
Equip Thy church to spread the light.

Bessie P. Head (*c.* 1914)
(298, *Anglican Hymn Book*)

'O Breath of Life, Come Sweeping through Us'

We end this week's reflections by looking at the words of this lovely hymn.

The Holy Spirit is like air, like oxygen – the breath of life. When God created the world, he breathed life into his creation. When the Holy Spirit came, he brought the life of the Spirit to dwell in us. Are we a fit dwelling? We know

66

that on our own we are not, and we cry out to the Holy Spirit to cleanse us in every part. We know the power of the Holy Spirit to transform us, to give us new life. When Jesus came, he came to bring us life, and that we might have it abundantly! This abundant life is breathed in us through his Holy Spirit. It's a kind of holy CPR, bringing us back from death.

As Jesus told Nicodemus, it is the Spirit who gives life, regenerating our dead inner human spirit and making it responsive to the life of God (John 3.5–6). The Holy Spirit comes as our teacher, our helper and our guide, to strengthen us and make us holy.

The first verse of this hymn expresses our longing to be made clean, to be made strong again, to be filled with life and power. Like Peter's mother-in-law we long to be made fit to serve, not just as individuals, but as the Body of Christ on earth, his Church.

Maybe we are weakened by sickness or disappointment, paralysed by disobedience or fear, perhaps we are dis-empowered by sin and shame, or unable to see the way ahead. Then, the healing reviving touch of Jesus Christ and the transforming strength of the Holy Spirit can fit us again for the loving service he has called us to from the beginning. Powerlessness has often made individuals and churches weak in worship, witness and service. Our churches need to be filled with renewed Christians, revived and enlivened 'to meet this hour'. This Advent we can begin to be those people so that this Christmas celebration is the greatest our church has seen, and so that we will be ready when Christ returns in Glory.

How can we welcome in the Holy Spirit's transforming power?

The second verse says: '*O wind of God, come bend us, break us.*' In Acts 2.1–7, we can see that the Holy wind of God has the power to blow away preconceptions, fears, uncertainties and fill us with new courage and purpose.

At this time of year, particularly in Yorkshire, we are very aware of the power of the wind. Sometimes, if we step out to go for a walk when the wind is at its height, we may have to bend double to make any headway, we may even risk being blown on a course we hadn't planned. We need to be ready for the wind of God to challenge our own strength and turn us onto the right path. If we try to battle the wind, we make no progress, but if we turn around so that the wind is behind us, we will go faster than we thought possible. Yet being buffeted by the wind can be exhausting. We need that wonderful lull of peace we experience when we find shelter, to reassess where we are and where we should be going. There we will find peace with God, and allow him to remake us in his image, make us holy as he is holy, and ready us to begin again on our journey in his strength.

In Verse 3 we plead, '*O Breath of love, come breathe within us*'. The Holy Spirit imparts gifts and the greatest of these gifts is love: 'there is nothing love cannot face; there is no limit to its faith, its hope, its endurance' – as the Apostle Paul says in his letter to the Corinthians (1 Corinthians 13.7).

Even if we have to endure suffering, St Paul tells us, we can 'exult in the hope of the divine glory that is to be ours. [3]More than this: we even exult in our present sufferings, because we know that suffering is a source of endurance, [4]endurance of approval, and approval of hope. [5]Such hope is no fantasy; through the Holy Spirit he has given us, God's love has flooded our hearts' (Romans 5.2b–5).

The breath of love, which the Holy Spirit breathes into us – inhabiting our hearts and minds – joins us inseparably to our loving Lord, and makes us more Christlike.

As I think of the careful and beautiful restoration and renewal of God's people, through the Holy Spirit, I am reminded of the immense work which has been going on in York Minster. A ten-year programme of restoration of the magnificent East Window was completed last year. This 600-year-old window, the size of a tennis court, with 311 panes of glass, was meticulously removed, the damaged glass cleaned, repaired and restored before being put back. The restorers spent around 92,500 hours conserving and restoring the glass. What an amazing job. In addition to the glasswork there is constant preservation and repair of the stonework. In the restoration project about 2,500 stones have been cut or repaired by stonemasons. I remember speaking to one of the apprentice stonemasons when I visited the stone yard. I asked him where the stone he was carving was destined to be put. He replied that it would go at the top of one of the windows, just below the roof. 'But no one will see your work', I exclaimed. He replied, 'I know, but I hope that in a hundred years when it is being repaired again, another stonemason will see it and think the work was good.'

When the Holy Spirit renews and restores us, may we trust that our restoration endures, and that when he returns, the original architect will see that it is good.

Prayer

Holy Spirit, come and blow all the uncleanness that clings to us and keeps us from you; remake us in your image – new every morning to do your will, and fill us with your love so that we can share your healing cleansing love with others. Amen.

Reflection

Think about your church this Advent and Christmas. In what ways might it be cleansed, renewed and remade so that Jesus Christ's love shines out to those who enter it this Christmas?

WEEK 3: FEED UP!

Collect for the Third Sunday of Advent

> Blessed Lord, who caused all holy scriptures to be written for our learning: help us so to hear them, to read, mark, learn and inwardly digest them that, through patience, and the comfort of your holy word, we may embrace and for ever hold fast the hope of everlasting life, which you have given us in our Saviour Jesus Christ, who is alive and reigns with you, in the unity of the Holy Spirit, one God, now and for ever.

What a wonderful prayer as we begin this Third Week of Advent. It is the prayer for Bible Sunday (which now in the Church's calendar and for the Bible Society is the last Sunday after Trinity) which some of you may have celebrated at the end of October. But it is still the Collect for the Second Sunday of Advent in the Book of Common Prayer of 1662. Given this week's theme of 'Feed Up' I believe this Collect gathers and sums up what this week of study and reflection will reveal to us.

Reading this Collect for Bible Sunday, our hearts are warmed by the Subject of all Holy Scriptures, God and His love affair with humankind, the promise of redemption and forgiveness, and the Good News of our salvation. These words are food enough for us. But inwardly digested in bite-size chunks while treating Holy Scripture as a whole and the whole of Holy Scripture.

In the last two weeks we have been looking at how we prepare to greet our Saviour now, and when he Comes Again. As we imagine the start of a new day, we have been looking at how we must *Wake Up*, and *Clean Up* in order to be ready. This week we are looking at the next step of our morning preparations – *Feeding Up*. Having arisen from the darkness, dressed and cleaned, we then turn to nourishing our souls and bodies. This collect encourages us to take in and digest God's Word each day so that we might know implicitly *the hope of everlasting life given to us in our Saviour Jesus Christ.*

THIRD SUNDAY OF ADVENT

Feed Up on God's Word (John 1.1–5, 14)

[1]In the beginning the Word already was. The Word was in God's presence, and what God was, the Word was. [2]He was with God at the beginning, [3]and through him all things came to be; without him no created thing came into being. [4]In him was life, and that life was the light of mankind. [5]The light shines in the darkness, and the darkness has never mastered it. [14]So the Word became flesh; he made his home among us, and we saw his glory, such glory as befit the Father's only Son, full of grace and truth.

I can never read or hear those words without picturing two things.

First, the darkness of a church or cathedral, pierced only by the light of candles, as we begin that glorious Christmas service of Nine Lessons and Carols.

Second, the darkness of the uncreated heavens, as the great Word is spoken into the void, bringing order, light and life into being. That Word, reverberating through the ages, making and remaking all things, is

72

still echoing in the universe, and living in all that we see and experience.

And with the birth of Jesus Christ, that great Word took on human flesh – Emmanuel, God with us. The Word, who spoke life into the void, comes to meet us, in order to give us eternal life in him.

Yes, at Christmas we remember the Word of Life made flesh – as God with us, Jesus of Nazareth sharing our human existence, teaching and feeding his disciples both with the miraculous bread in the crowds around Galilee, and with the love and wisdom of his teaching.

And as we pray the Bible Sunday prayer, we also celebrate the Word of Life which has come to us in Scripture throughout the ages, helping us to be fed and nourished by the knowledge of his truth.

In that way, the Word becomes flesh in our own lives through the work of the Holy Spirit in us.

The Word which was with God in the beginning, which was God, is living in us. What an amazing thought. And since he is the Word dwelling in our flesh through the Holy Spirit, we must become *speakers* of the Word. The Word needs to be spoken. As Jesus said to the carping religious leaders on Palm Sunday, 'if my disciples are silent the stones will shout aloud' (Luke 19.40).

The Word of God is our daily food, we are being fed and nurtured through his presence and strength. Because our theme for this week is 'Feeding Up', I'd like to consider some of the ways we are fed.

I was born at 3 a.m. in Mengo Missionary Hospital, Kampala, on the 10 June 1949. I weighed only four pounds, and on the first/index finger of my tiny right hand was a transparent membrane covering a dark fluid – this was later used to register my birth. Dr Billington didn't think I would make it by daybreak. So he sent a nurse to wake up the Bishop of Namirembe to come and baptize me. I was baptized Sentamu.

Three weeks later my mum was allowed to take me home. A neighbour came around to see the sixth child of the local headmaster and Catechist. The neighbour, a friend of the family, is reputed to have said to my mum, 'Tiny little rat!'

I was in and out of hospital for ten years. Dr Billington told my parents that if I made it to my tenth birthday, I would grow into adulthood – though many life challenges would lie ahead of me.

I made it. That tenth birthday is indelibly written on my mind. Because Hugh Silvester, a teacher, led me to Christ at my birthday celebration. I was overwhelmed by the joy of encountering Christ. No one could stop me from sharing the love of Christ welling up inside me.

I survived and thrived. I did need feeding up but so do we all. I was fortunate, because my parents not only fed me well (including the 15 of us plus many visitors), but they also fed me with God's words of love and care, with stories of Jesus and the hope of his promises. I became strong and healthy in body and spirit.

The Word of God will give us the food our soul needs, so how can we feed ourselves and each other up, so that we can be made fit as citizens of the Rule of God? The Bible Sunday prayer gives us a pattern to follow:

1 By *hearing the Word of God*, in church and in meetings, in the company of our Christian brothers and sisters.
2 By *reading the Word of God* and holding it in our hearts.

3 By *marking the Word of God* – that is to say, paying attention, heeding what God is telling us through his word, and considering how this should inform our actions. The Holy Spirit enlivens the Word of God for us.

4 By *learning the Word of God* – having the words of eternal life always at hand in our hearts and minds to help us bring God into every situation. Creating habits of the heart that are obedient.

5 By *digesting the Word of God* – digestion is the whole point of eating. Through our inward digestion the raw ingredients of what we take in are transformed into the vital nutrients our body needs for health and growth. So it is as we digest the Word of God, the nourishing truths of God feed our souls and build us up; and we become what we eat, God bearers. As the Psalmist says, 'I treasure your promise in my heart, for fear that I might sin against you' (Psalm 119.11). 'How sweet is your promise to my palate, sweeter on my tongue than honey!' (Psalm 119.103), 'More to be desired, than gold; pure gold in plenty, sweeter than honey dripping from the comb' (Psalm 19.10).

We must follow this pattern patiently and humbly, being ever ready to be taught, reproved, corrected and encouraged as we learn and grow.

Yet two more things are needed.

We must *Act on the Word* and not just listen, so says James:

²¹Then discard everything sordid, and every wicked excess, and meekly accept the message planted in your

hearts, with its power to save you. [22]Only be sure you act on the message, and do not merely listen and so deceive yourselves. [23]Anyone who listens to the message but does not act on it is like somebody looking in a mirror at the face nature gave him; [24]he glances at himself and goes his way, and promptly forgets what he looked like. [25]But he who looks into the perfect law, the law that makes us free, and does not turn away, remembers what he hears; he acts on it, and by so acting he will find happiness.

(James 1.21–25)

And we must be *Speakers of the Word* – as I mentioned earlier. The Word is living in us and must be shared with others:

[16]Let the gospel of Christ dwell among you in all its richness; teach and instruct one another with all the wisdom it gives you. With psalms and hymns and spiritual songs, sing from the heart in gratitude to God. [17]Let every word and action, everything you do, be in the name of the Lord Jesus, and give thanks through him to God the Father. (Colossians 3.16–17)

Prayer

Let us pray again the prayer for Bible Sunday we read at the beginning:

Blessed Lord, who caused all holy scriptures to be written for our learning: help us so to hear them, to read, mark, learn and inwardly digest them that, through patience, and the comfort of your holy word, we may embrace and for ever hold fast the hope of everlasting life, which you have given us in our Saviour Jesus Christ, who is alive and reigns with you, in the unity of the Holy Spirit, one God, now and for ever. Amen.

Reflection

Think about the food you have eaten today. How much of it was nourishing? Are there elements in what you have eaten that might have done you harm? What are your plans for eating over the coming days? Is there any way of making any healthy changes? Spare a thought and take action for those going hungry today.

WEEK 3: MONDAY

Feed Up for Ever (John 6.25–27, 33–35)

[25]They found him on the other side. 'Rabbi', they asked, 'when did you come here?' [26]Jesus replied, 'In very truth I tell you, it is not because you saw signs that you came looking for me, but because you ate the bread and your hunger was satisfied. [27]You should work, not for this perishable food, but for the food that lasts, the food of eternal life.

'This food the Son of Man will give you, for on him God the Father has set the seal of his authority.'

[33]The bread that God gives comes down from heaven and brings life to the world.' [34]"Sir', they said to him, 'give us this bread now and always.' [35]Jesus said to them, 'I am the bread of life. Whoever comes to me will never be hungry, and whoever believes in me will never be thirsty'.

I read recently that in the UK alone we throw away the equivalent of 24 million slices of bread every day! Against the background of hunger and deprivation, ours is still a throw-away culture. We don't expect things to last; in fact, we often don't want them to. We are novelty-seekers, always wanting the next fashion item, the newest technology, the next exciting big thing. Jesus was challenging the crowd who seemed to see him as 'the next big thing' in prophets. He had miraculously fed the crowd; and now they want their friends to see a repeat of this amazing performance. But Jesus tells them to refocus. What you want is just a 'here today and gone tomorrow' experience, he says. Focus on something whose effects will last. Something which will touch you deeply and bring new and lasting nourishment and strength in all you do. Something only the Son of Man can bring – for 'it is on him that God the Father has set his seal' (i.e. His Deed of Authorization). This will provide a lasting, eternal, life-giving diet – certified as 100 per cent wholesome by the Maker. 'Accept no substitutes.'

As Jesus continues to speak to the crowd, he develops the idea of a new kind of bread. What he is bringing to the world is beyond the miracle of the heavenly bread their ancestors received in the desert. A fine and flaky food, as fine as frost on the ground. On seeing this they said, 'What is it?' Moses replied to their question 'What is it?' by saying, 'That is the bread which the Lord has given you to eat' (Exodus 16.15b). So they named it *manna* – for it was like coriander seed, white, 'and it tasted like wafers made with honey' (Exodus 16.31).

This bread is not just something to keep us alive from one day to the next. It is the food of eternal life. If 'we are what we eat', then eating the bread that Jesus provides by his own body will truly make us his brothers and sisters, and the children of God the Father. In this way, we are united to Christ and become children of an eternal family.

'A food that doesn't perish or go off.' That is the food which Jesus offers. It is not like our long-lasting bread which takes time to go stale because of the additives. The bread that Jesus offers is, in its very essence, imperishable because it comes from his eternal life. It has no sell-by date.

In speaking of this bread, Jesus echoes the prophecy of Isaiah 55, which we shall be reading tomorrow. For now, accepting this bread of life – freely given – gives us life.

When children are growing up and learning to eat new things, they often push their food away, untried, saying, 'I don't like that.' They need to discover by experience how good it tastes. Yet during their 'faddy' phase, parents will tell their children, 'Remember there are people in the world who don't have enough to eat. Feed up and be thankful.' Regaling similar stories to our children produced faces which seemed to say, 'What planet are you on?'

Every day we see images of people perishing from physical hunger, suffering famines which are often brought about as a result of greed, war, oppression or natural hazards. Yet if we look around us closely and with the compassionate gaze of our heavenly Father, we will also see people who are perishing from spiritual hunger. So, if we are tempted to turn away from the living bread of Christ, let us remind ourselves that there are many people in the world who are dying for lack of just a few crumbs of that bread of hope and life.

The bread that Jesus Christ offers is sufficient for all our needs and not our greeds! As I said yesterday, when we eat and digest we take in the nutrients which build up our health and strength, and pass out what is of no use as waste. With the living bread of Jesus Christ, nothing is wasted. Everything we eat and digest is for our eternal life.

Every Word of God is food for our soul. That is why, when we eat of the Bread of Life, we need never be hungry, and if we believe and know the presence of Jesus Christ in our lives we will never be thirsty. Because the property of the bread that satisfies is that it transforms the person so that they experience what 'being satisfied' feels like.

Jesus is the bread of life. In Uganda (among the Bantu tribes generally), bananas are the staple diet, like rice in some countries, and like bread here in the UK. Jesus gives us the bread, the banana, the rice of life; which means that he is essential for life. Therefore, to refuse the invitation and command of Jesus is to miss life and go unnecessarily hungry – if we are hungry and thirst for meaning.

The Greek word used for 'life' in these verses is not just 'existence'. It's a word which means a quality of life, an experience of life that finds its source in God. It is what we might understand by Jesus Christ's reference to 'life in all its fullness' – 'abundant life'.

This is a life given by the living bread, not by the sanitised, plastic wrapped bread on the supermarket shelves, or even the more charming (and expensive) 'artisan bread' in the upmarket bakeries.

I remember an unforgettable celebration and challenge filled with simplicity, joy and compassion. Mother Teresa of Calcutta visited Cambridge University in 1975 to receive an Honorary Doctorate and deliver a lecture on poverty. The frail body of this Albanian nun climbed upon the platform to rapturous applause. When the clapping had died down she said, 'In the West, one of the greatest problems is loneliness. People die alone. You have the greatest evidence of poverty. Poverty of the spirit. It can only be fed by the bread of heaven: Jesus Christ. In India our greatest problem is togetherness. Diseases are easily shared but hardly any dies alone. We have the greatest evidence of poverty. Physical poverty. It can only be fed by the bread of heaven: Jesus Christ.'

Out of a cloth satchel she took out a loaf of bread, broke it in half, passed it on and said, 'Share it, and go and do likewise,' and she descended from the platform. I encourage you to do the same. Share Christ the bread of life: he is essential for life – essential for every man, woman, boy and girl –to enjoy life in all its abundance.

'Blessed are you who are poor, for yours is the Kingdom of God.'

Prayer

Jesus Christ, Son of the Father, born in a stable, by your poverty help us this Advent, to focus on what will bring lasting joy and health to our lives. Holy Spirit make us ready to share this 'bread' with others, that they too may have life in all its fullness. Amen

Reflection

When we next shop for bread in the supermarket, look at the aisles of different kinds of bread, and remind yourself that that bread is a very simple basic universal foodstuff, which should be available to even the very poorest. Remember that Jesus was telling the crowd that what he was offering was not just for the wealthy, privileged members of society. His offer was a gift of life-giving nourishment for the whole of humankind. Look around you and see what you might do, both for those who are physically hungry, and for those who are spiritually starving.

WEEK 3: TUESDAY

Feed Up for Free (Isaiah 55.1–3a, 6–7)

Come for water, all who are thirsty; though you have no money, come, buy grain and eat; come buy wine and milk, not for money, not for a price. ²Why spend your money for what is not food, your earnings on what fails to satisfy? Listen to me and you will fare well, you will enjoy the fat of the land. ³Come to me and listen to my words, hear me and you will have life.

⁶Seek the LORD while he is present, call to him while he is close at hand. ⁷Let the wicked abandon their ways and the evil their thoughts: let them return to the LORD, who will take pity on them, and to our God, for he will freely forgive.

While we are compiling our shopping lists for gifts and food for the Christmas celebrations, checking our bank balance to see whether it will hold up under the strain, let's consider God's invitation in Isaiah 55.

As we read those first words of the invitation in Isaiah's prophecy, 'Why do you spend your money for that which is not bread, and your labour for that which does not satisfy' (Isaiah 55.2 NRSV), we hear an echo of the words of Jesus speaking to the crowd in the passage we read yesterday. 'You should work, not for this perishable food, but for the food that lasts, the food of eternal life.'

What are we spending our money on this Christmas? What are we working hard for? Are we wasting our time and effort, when all that we truly need, for what is important in our life, can be had for the asking?

Simple wholesome fare, bought without money, is probably not what we've got in our supermarket trolleys when we're stocking up for Christmas. Here in the One-Third World, our baskets are more likely to be groaning with turkeys, beef, ham, chocolate, cream, cakes and biscuits, wine and spirits. You and your family may, even now, be working your way through the chocolate day-by-day in your Real Advent Calendar.

Thinking about food, reading about food, watching people cook food, seems to be a passion for many people in this country. In fact, a survey has found that Britons now spend more than five hours a week consuming 'food media', but only four hours actually cooking! A large percentage of the Christmas presents we give or receive will probably be cookery books written by celebrity chefs. And, of course, in the New Year, there will probably be a rush for diet books, slimming programmes and gym memberships.

I love to cook, but throughout the year I don't have time to do it as often as I would like. So, each year, at Christmas, I invite all the staff working across the Diocese for a carol service here at Bishopthorpe Palace, and I cook dinner. Last year 104 staff attended. Tomorrow we are expecting even more!

Yes, hospitality and celebration are all part of our Christmas tradition and it is good to reflect God's hospitality when we reach out and open our homes at this time of year. I have a motto for my ministry discernible from Jesus of Nazareth: *Prayer and Parties!*

Yet God's gracious summons in this passage has a far greater scope than anything we can provide. God's invitation has a much wider reach, a deeper dimension and a higher purpose. This is a trumpet call, a Special Offer, for the whole world. Not 'Buy One Get One Free' or

'Three for the Price of Two', but 'Buy for No Money', 'Feed Up and Be Satisfied'.

If we take up this offer, we will be fed with the ideal balanced diet, which has the perfect nutritional value for anyone and everyone.

God bids each one of us to come. His invitation is urgent and full of imperatives. Listen again to how he calls us:

> Come
> Buy
> Eat
> Listen
> Seek
> Return to the Lord

Come!

Who should come? Everyone is invited. All those who are thirsty and hungry and recognize their need can come. The poor, the destitute, those with nothing, as well as the comfortable and the wealthy can come. The proud, the humble, the righteous and the unrighteous. All are invited. They will all be provided with the same banquet. All they have to do is Come. His invitation is like a bag of sweets: *Allsorts*!

Buy with no money and without price!

When we are invited out to dinner, we quite often take some gift to show our appreciation for the hospitality. But this is different. Everyone – rich and poor alike – should come empty-handed. For none of us has anything to offer the King except our hunger and thirst.

We are asked to buy with no money, something without price. What can this be other than the priceless Love and Generosity of God, his saving grace and forgiveness, his gift of everlasting life. I'll buy that! Though all that I could give would be worthless – me. I will enter into that relationship of love and acceptance that's offered freely.

Eat What Is Good!

Take in God's word, and make it part of your daily nutrition. Feed on that.

Don't try to assuage your hunger with things that don't satisfy – that which isn't the living Bread. You can't fill the void with money, or sex or drugs or fame. What you are hungry for can only be found in the Water of Life, and the Bread of Life. Have whatever you hunger for from God and you will live.

Listen that You Might Live!

Incline your ear to hear God's word to you. Pay attention to what God is teaching you through your reading of the Bible, your prayers, the words of wisdom from friends, hymns and songs you sing together. These are the words of eternal life – don't be distracted by things that have a passing appeal.

Seek the Lord while He May Be Found!

Be careful that you don't treat this invitation carelessly. Remember the warning Jesus gave about the guests invited to the Great Banquet, which we read last week.

Those who turned down the King's invitation missed their opportunity and didn't get another. If we receive this invitation from God, would we say, as those guests did, that our own work, our holiday, even our family is more important? There is a sense of urgency in this invitation, because it really is a matter of our eternal life and death. Let us also not turn up in a spirit of 'take it or leave it' like the person who did not bother to go home and change into his best clothes. Challenged, he could not defend himself. He knew it.

Repent

I hope many of you will be invited to a meal, and that you will be given a gift this Christmas. When you are, you will no doubt write a thank you letter, or a card or a quick text in response.

Our response to Christ's invitation is to *repent (turn around from our mistaken ways to Christ's Way) and return to the Lord.*

Choosing to eat and drink of the Lord's bounty, rather than deciding to turn away from the Holy Spirit's invitation and thereby die of spiritual hunger and thirst. Let us return to Him. For he will abundantly pardon, and we will enjoy his promised life in all its fullness.

Prayer

Generous God, give us responsive hearts to hear your invitation to come and eat freely of your bounty. And give us repentant hearts that keep turning to you, so that we may know the abundant life that you offer us in your beloved Son. Amen.

Reflection

Think about the money you are spending, and how much of it is for things that bring life. Think about the things you can get for free, and whether they are life-transfiguring.

WEEK 3: WEDNESDAY

Feed Up in Obedience (Psalm 119.101–105)

I have kept your precepts.
[101]I do not set foot on any evil path in my obedience to your word; [102]I do not swerve from your decrees, for you have been my teacher. [103]How sweet is your promise to my palate, sweeter on my tongue than honey! [104]From your precepts I learn wisdom; therefore I hate every path of falsehood.
[105]Your word is a lamp to my feet, a light on my path.

What a remarkable chapter of the Bible is Psalm 119. Not only because it's the longest, not only because it's written in the form of a poem with each verse beginning with a letter of the Hebrew alphabet in correct sequence, but because it is a hymn of praise to the Law.

We people of the New Covenant are sometimes tempted to forget that Jesus did not come to abolish the Law. He came to show how full of love and wisdom and care for our well-being God's law is when it is received and understood by humble hearts.

The final verse of today's passage, '[105]Your word is a lamp to my feet, a light on my path', is significant in explaining why the Psalmist loves and desires to follow the Law. In the first week of this Study, we looked at the perils and dangers of this present darkness. Today we continue to reflect on our need for God's help. The Third Collect, For Aid Against All Perils, at Evening Prayer, expresses our need succinctly: 'Lighten our darkness, Lord, we pray; and in your mercy defend us from all perils and dangers of this night; for the love of your only Son, our Saviour Jesus Christ. Amen.'

Throughout Psalm 119 there are eight different words used to illuminate all the different parts of God's Law which the Psalmist loves and honours. They are:

- *commandment* – reflecting our Covenant relationship with God;
- *law* – Judicial Law, Ceremonial Law, as well as Moral Law;
- ordinance/judgement – how God's law is applied in every circumstance;
- *precept* – the responsibility laid on those in a relationship with God;
- *statute/regulations* – the conditions for observance of the law;
- *testimony* – the corroboration of the truth of God's Word, by personal witness;
- *way/road* – God's path, or the path to destruction;
- *word* – what is spoken by God, and of course in the New Testament as well as the whole testimony and life of Jesus Christ.

If you reflect on these words, you will see that they cover all of Scripture. Each chapter of God's love story with humankind can be found here. No wonder the psalmist loves the Word of God as it comes through these elements.

In those few short verses of our passage today, we read

of four of these parts of the Law – God's path, his word, his judgements and his precepts. The Psalmist takes care to keep his feet from wandering onto an evil way, but in listening and obeying God's word he remains safe. He is not distracted or tempted to turn off this path, away from God's ordinances, because God has taught him, and he has learnt to obey and follow. And he has learnt to hate and distrust the false way which comes from refusing the responsibility that his love for God has laid on him – God's precepts.

There is a knowledge that comes only from obedience. Wisdom comes from learning to turn away from temptation in the strength of God's Word as Jesus found during his forty days in the wilderness, fasting and being led by the Holy Spirit. At the end of this time he was famished and the devil offered three priorities to Jesus: (i) a sort of *humanitarianism* or programme of helping people in need in which God would probably get left out; (ii) a sort of *supernaturalism*, in which Jesus would only be concerned with making a big impression and in which God might easily get left out; and (iii) a sort of *secularization* or involvement in the world in which God would certainly get left out.

Jesus was committed to the right sort of humanitarian aid, the supernatural demonstration of God's rule on earth, and the right engagement with the world. But as his basic principle of action, Jesus stuck to the priority of God the Father's will and word. That alone, he knew, would enable him not simply to do what the world wanted him to, but also what he himself wanted to do. Having this priority led him to a life of living sacrifice to the Cross. Jesus Christ is our best companion in the fight against temptation.

In that vulnerable isolation, away from his family, and

his community, and facing the challenge of what he was called to do, Jesus of Nazareth was able to resist robustly the Enemy by calling to his aid the Word of God, the Law, that was living in him and permeating his every thought and action.

'Man shall not live by bread alone, but by every word that proceeds from the mouth of God' (Matthew 4.4 RSV) – so Jesus tells the tempter when he tempts him because Jesus is famished – quoting Deuteronomy (8.3).

He next trumps the devil's misuse of Scripture, as he tempts him to take the way of pride and grasping. Jesus replies, 'Scripture also says, "You are not to put the Lord your God to the test" ' – quoting this time Deuteronomy 6.16 and leaving out the words, 'as you did at Massah'.

Finally, when the devil calls on Jesus to seek personal power, and give up his allegiance to God the Father, Jesus responds with all the power of the Law, the first and greatest Commandment: 'Begone, Satan! for it is written, "You shall worship the Lord your God, and him only shall you serve"' (Matthew 4.10 RSV, quoting Deuteronomy 6.13).

The Word of God brings us knowledge, wisdom, safety. Why would we not love it? And then, God's word is a delight. It is better than all kinds of fine food, things which attract the eye and the senses. There is no other sweetness on earth like the pleasure God's word gives – and it's not passing pleasure, it's eternal. Honey was probably the sweetest thing the psalmist had ever tasted. Today, in our part of the world, we have our pick of an overabundance of sweet things, but God's word is not only sweeter, it is more wholesome, more nourishing, more health-giving. His Word gives us discernment.

Watching food or wine buffs on television I am often

struck by their expressions of delight over a particular flavour or aroma. Their senses are so trained and heightened that they can discern a hint of some special herb or spice or essential flavour that makes a dish stand out, but which coarser palates would miss. Similarly, with wine. Experts can tell where a wine grape originates, even down to a particular section of a vineyard. Those with such fine judgement are willing to pay far more than the rest of us could afford to enjoy what they find the best. But we are all privileged and can experience the best taste of all, which God offers to us free of charge.

This Advent, as we contemplate the coming of the Word made Flesh among us, can we say, with the psalmist, 'How I love your law, how I love your word!'? Can we take comfort and delight in knowing that we can 'restrain our feet' from going the wrong way? Can we feed on God's Word, make it part of us, so that we, like Jesus of Nazareth, can resist turning away from God the Maker's Instruction? Can we rejoice in the delight of knowing we are safe on the right way, that we are held firm by something we know is right, something that is in the purposes of God for our lives?

Prayer

God of the Law of Life, help us this Advent to prepare ourselves for the feast, and in obedience come to you and taste, eat, and see how gracious the Lord is. How sweet is your word, O Lord. Amen.

Reflection

Earlier this month, I was listening to that beautiful Vaughan Williams setting of Psalm 34, which he wrote for the coronation of Queen Elizabeth II in 1953. The choir's soaring voices invited us to:

> O taste and see how gracious the Lord is.
> Blessed is the man
> that trusteth in him!

Let us think of how God is graciously helping us to learn this Advent. Let us think about how he is blessing us.

WEEK 3: THURSDAY

Feed Up Young Minds (Psalm 119.9–16)

[9]How may a young man lead a clean life? By holding to your words. [10]With all my heart I seek you; do not let me stray from your commandments.[11]I treasure your promise in my heart for fear that I might sin against you. [12]Blessed are you, LORD; teach me your statutes. [13]I say them over, one by one, all the decrees you have announced. [14]I have rejoiced in the path of your instructions as one rejoices over wealth of every kind. [15]I shall meditate on your precepts and keep your paths before my eyes. [16]In your statutes I find continual delight; I shall not forget your word.

Over the last year the country has become increasingly concerned by the troubles and dangers facing our young people, perils which are often irreparably damaging their lives.

In the face of the stress of 24-hour access to social media, exposure to negative images and bullying, anxiety about failure at school or in the job market, family breakdown, drug and alcohol abuse, and of course the major problem of knife crime and fear on the streets, we may in these hazardous days echo the question of the psalmist with heartfelt emphasis.

It is usually a question addressed to educationalists and the police: How can these risks to our young people be avoided? How can they be kept safe and secure? There has, as yet, been no clear answer. The problem is fraught with difficulty, and when the young people themselves are asked the question, they are at a loss. Fear, helplessness, even despair, keep them captive.

Sometimes we are heartened by stories of young people who have come through these times of difficulty. Many, having themselves turned the corner and found a way to safety, are giving their time and energy to provide positive examples of action and help for other young people. They model ways in which young people under threat can take responsibility for choosing a better, safer path.

It is an age-old issue, not just a modern one. The psalmist is asking the same question – 'how can young people keep their way pure'? And in the context of his hymn of praise to the all-encompassing truth of the Law, it is to the saving elements of God's Word that he directs his answer.

You may think that Psalm 119 would not be the first-choice chapter for use in a Youth Group Bible Study. Young people like to learn through action, through relating their reading to real-life situations in their lives. They're not usually too keen on lists of rules, directions, at an age when rebellion and questioning come more naturally than obedience.

Let's look again at those verses in today's passage. There

are clearly a number of decisions and actions which young people might want to take to ensure they are on the right track.

Life is an adventure with many challenges. Finding a moral compass and a gracious anchor is a vital skill for young people – looking carefully at the way they are going, and checking it against the way God has called them to be (vv 9–10).

The enthusiasm of young people means that when they have recognized the virtue of something they are ready to embrace it and share it. A negligent, careless, procrastinating response will not keep them safe.

They need to be determined and intentional. Once they love and delight in the truth of God's Word as being necessary for life they are ready to share it fearlessly.

Many young people who have made good decisions are ready to stand up and speak against, say, an easy acceptance of racism, gender discrimination, misuse (or neglect) of the environment, hateful talk, pressures on image or of money. When they feel passionately about something they don't hold back – they will share their views on Twitter, Facebook, Instagram, texts, whatever their favourite form of communication is (vv. 12–14).

Yet there are always temptations, and they need the discipline of deep thinking so that they remember the truth of what they have learnt. When they are younger, children like the challenge of learning memory verses. These words will be lodged in their hearts as they grow up, giving them strength to draw on when they need it.

It is interesting to know that some great leaders in the past were actually set the task of learning Psalm 119 and came to value its effect on their lives:

- David Livingstone, intrepid explorer and missionary to Africa, learnt the Psalm when he was nine.
- William Wilberforce, who as a politician played a major role in the abolition of the slave trade, speaks of memorizing and reciting the psalm as he walked to work.
- John Ruskin, a writer, art critic and social reformer, recognized that the psalm which as a child he had found so difficult became the most precious to him.

All the guidance and direction in this Psalm are part of the nourishment which will help young people grow into strong, honourable adults. Young people as they grow, seem always to be hungry. They need the right food if they are to flourish – and that means the right spiritual food, as well as the physical three square-meals a day.

Not all young people are fortunate enough to have a balanced diet, and this can result in them falling short in their growth and development – failing to flourish.

Teachers and carers of young people have frequently expressed concern that if the children come to school without having eaten properly they will be less likely to learn, to thrive, to progress, and their future chances will be impaired.

That's why breakfast clubs have been set up, so that those who were not getting a proper diet could be given the necessary advantages to help them flourish.

Back in 2005, you may remember that Jamie Oliver began his campaign to encourage healthy eating for children – 'Jamie's School Meals'. It was quite a controversial programme at the time and met with considerable criticism from all quarters – food writers as well as children and parents. But he countered the criticism, saying, 'A poor diet might not sound as scary as murder or terrorism, but it's much more likely to kill you.'

Research from the University of London's Centre for Educational Neuroscience[1] has demonstrated that an inadequate diet has a detrimental effect on the potential of young people as they attempt to grow in stature and wisdom. It is damaging to their achieving their hopes and aspirations.

The psalmist also makes us aware that young people who are malnourished spiritually are in danger of poor spiritual growth. Our eternal health and safety are at stake.

It was because of my awareness of the challenges for our Young People that I set up The Archbishop of York's Youth Trust in 2008. I announced then that my vision was that, rather than being part of the problem facing some of our communities today, young people were actually the answer. Over the past eleven years, the charity has been helping them show their potential – 'to be the change they want to see'. We have reached out to thousands of young people through the Youth Leadership scheme in schools, and our Young Leaders Awards have empowered some 73,000 young people in over 600 schools to serve in their local communities. These Awards recognize and celebrate what young people have to offer.

What they learn in the programme nourishes them, gives them the strength and stature to take on the responsibility of leadership roles in their communities. They are like the young person in the Psalm who has

---

1 http://www.educationalneuroscience.org.uk/resources/neuromyth-or-neuro-fact/diet-makes-a-difference-to-learning/

accepted the discipline of God's Word and has grown in maturity and wisdom.

Just over six months ago, in May this year, we had a splendid coming together of the feeding of the body and the feeding of our young people's potential in a grand Charity Dinner at Bowcliffe Hall here in Yorkshire. It was a heavenly banquet cooked up by Mary Berry and Frances Atkins to raise money for the work of the Youth Trust.

I pray that through this work we will continue to find ways of feeding bodies, minds and spirits of many more young people, so that we may all benefit from the change our young people can offer in our world.

Prayer

Jesus Christ, our Teacher and Master, bless all those called to serve you in caring and nurturing our young people. May they share with the young people in their care the same good food which has nurtured them. Amen.

Reflection

Think about the young people you know. What are their favoured means of learning and communication? Are there ways in which they can be encouraged to gossip the gospel throughout cyberspace? Are there ways in which you can support youth work/mentoring in your church or community?

WEEK 3: FRIDAY

Feed Up for Strength (1 Kings 19.4–9)

³In fear he fled for his life, and when he reached Beersheba in Judah he left his servant there, ⁴while he himself went a day's journey into the wilderness. He came to a broom bush, and sitting down, under it he prayed for death: 'It is enough,' he said: 'now, LORD, take away my life, for I am no better than my fathers before me.' He lay down under the bush and, while he slept, an angel touched him and said, ⁶'Rise and eat.' He looked, and there at this head was a cake baked on hot stones, and a pitcher of water. He ate and drank and lay down again. ⁷The angel of the LORD came again and touched him a second time, saying, 'Rise and eat; the journey is too much for you.' ⁸He rose and ate and drank and, sustained by this food, he went on for forty days and forty nights to Horeb, the mount of God. ⁹There he entered a cave where he spent the night.

In these days of high-stress lifestyles, and with growing numbers of people suffering from depression and mental health problems, Elijah's response to his situation is probably quite recognizable.

Just before today's reading, Elijah had come through an episode of extremely high stress. Ahab, the King of Israel, and his wife Jezebel, had led the people of Israel into worshipping the false God, Baal. Elijah challenges Ahab and the 450 prophets of Baal with the 400 prophets of Asherah who were part of the Jezebel's court to prove their god's power. In this encounter, the followers of Baal were humiliated, and Elijah conclusively demonstrated the overwhelming authority of the True God over all things.

That was stress, but it was exhilarating stress. Elijah was high on adrenalin, we might say, as he left Mount Carmel.

Then he heard that the Queen Jezebel, enraged by the outcome, had issued a death sentence on him and, in verse three, we read 'In fear he fled for his life'.

It may seem strange to us that, having just seen the power of the Living God demonstrated in such a dramatic way, having known that he can call upon the Lord, and be heard and upheld, Elijah should then doubt and crumble so readily in the face of Jezebel's threats. He had faced down the king, and a huge crowd of antagonists, apparently alone – but with God's presence to sustain him. However, the threat of one enraged woman, even if that woman is a queen, is enough to break his nerve.

However, it is a recognized physical and mental reaction, that when you have been living in a state of high tension, when you are strung up, even when you are elated, your emotions can be unstable, and you are vulnerable and may be easily broken. Though we are followers of Jesus Christ, our Saviour, we too are not exempt from the consequences of physical and mental exhaustion. I am all too aware that many clergy, often feeling alone and under attack as they strive for the spiritual safety and care of their Cure of Souls, can fall into anxiety and depression. They, and others, whom we might expect always to find enough mental and physical strength in their faith can sometimes find that circumstances defeat them.

If you have read that wonderful book *Pilgrim's Progress* you may remember that Christian, the pilgrim journeying to the Glorious City together with his companion Hopeful, were taken by the Giant Despair and put into Doubting Castle. They are only delivered after a horrific fight in which Mr Great-heart, old Honest and four young men fight the Giant and his wife, Diffidence.

Despair and doubt are part of the battle that Christians, along with many others, fight each day.

Yet God is gracious and compassionate. He was gracious to Elijah as he is to us. He helps us to triumphs of faith, and he helps us when we fall into the 'Slough of Despond', that deep bog in *Pilgrim's Progress* where Christian sinks under the weight of his guilt and sin.

Let's look again at how God responds to Elijah's despair.

He doesn't rebuke us for our weakness. Although we, like Elijah, might moan and complain and wish we were dead, God sends encouragement, rest and food to build us up and lift our weariness from us.

It is interesting that doctors recommend five lifestyle changes to help reduce stress and boost resilience to fight depression:

1 sleep
2 good diet
3 strong supportive relationship
4 meditation or prayer
5 a restful break from routine.

God was ahead of them in his restoration of Elijah.

We read that Elijah *prayed* in his despair, and was given *sleep*. When he had slept, God came to him through the Angel of the Lord – a name often associated with a direct encounter with God. The angel brought *food and water*, and then Elijah was granted sleep again, perhaps a more restful sleep this time, following the heavenly sustenance he had received. Later the angel returns once more with *food and water.* This time the food sustains him for a *journey* which he is called to make – and in the strength of that food, Elijah is able to travel for forty days and forty nights until he reaches his destination, Horeb, the mountain of God. If we read on in 1 Kings Chapter 19, we see that this is the place where Elijah encounters God in '*a soft murmuring voice*' (1 Kings 19.12b). Not in *the strong wind* that split the mountains and broke the rocks in pieces; not in *the earthquake*; and not in *the fire*.

After all the excitement of the battle on Mount Carmel, after all the noise and fury of King Ahab and his prophets, and of Jezebel's response, Elijah hears again the call of God and this time in 'a soft murmuring voice'. Hearing it, Elijah wraps his face in his mantle, goes out and stands at the entrance of the cave. The commanding voice of God addresses him, and he goes on his way renewed and with a restored sense of proportion. He is not alone. He is indeed a prophet like Moses (cf. Deuteronomy 18.15, 18).

This week we have been considering the theme 'Feed Up' and we have seen the different ways in which God feeds and nourishes us – through his Word, through his invitation to his Great Banquet, through Jesus, the Living Bread. Tomorrow we will look at how we come together as we feed on Christ in the Sacrament and mystery of Holy Communion. But today we see that God will also meet us and feed us and nourish us in the depths of the fear, anger and sorrow that we experience in our lives. We see that he brings real strengthening rest and sustenance to restore us and help us as we continue on our journey. And we know that at the end of that journey we will meet with the Living God. Let us listen for that '*soft murmuring voice*' of his glory and power. Let us not wait for the high octane events or the sound effects which preceded God's presence before His encounters with Moses and Elijah.

Prayer

Lord God of love and power, bring your peace and quietness into our busy lives this Advent. Refresh us with the food of your Word, so that we can have strength for all that lies ahead. Amen.

Reflection

Consider the stresses and strains on your life, especially in this season. Are there ways in which you can simplify the burden on your time and energy? Are there ways in which you can help others bear the pressure? Consider whether the idea of having a simple Christmas is a possibility – this year, or next year?

WEEK 3: SATURDAY

Feed Up in Communion with God and One Another

1 Bread of heaven, on thee we feed,
for thy flesh is meat indeed;
ever may our souls be fed
with this true and living bread;
day by day with strength supplied
through the life of him who died.

2 Vine of heaven, thy blood supplies
this blest cup of sacrifice;
Lord, thy wounds our healing give,

to thy cross we look and live:
Jesus, may we ever be
grafted, rooted, built in thee.

Josiah Conder (1789–1855)

This wonderful Communion hymn has been a favourite in our churches for many years. It may be that it is not sung quite so often these days, but it beautifully sums up what Christ has done for us, what we are remembering each Sunday as we gather round the Holy Table, and the marvellous gift of heavenly life-giving food we have been considering this week.

As I mentioned in Monday's study, in the sacrament of Holy Communion we experience another foretaste, as well as a remembrance of God's self-giving hospitality. As Bishop John Jewel of Salisbury put it (in Latin in 1562: *Apologia Ecclesiae Anglicanae*, MDCVI),

By Partaking in the Communion of the Body and Blood of Christ, the Food of Immortality, Grace and Truth and Life – we are changed and transformed into Christ's body; Quickened, Strengthened, and Fed Unto Immortality, and by this we are Joined and Incorporated with Christ, so that we may *Abide in Him, and He in us.* The Lord's Supper is a Sacrament ... wherein the Death of Christ, and his Resurrection, and whatever he did in his flesh, is, in a manner, set before our Eyes; that we may give Thanks for his Death, and our Salvation; and, by the Frequent Receiving of the Sacrament, may continue a lively sense of it in our Minds; that we may be Nourished with the Body and Blood of Christ, unto the Hope of the Resurrection and Eternal Life; and may most assuredly

Believe that our Souls are fed with the *Body and Blood of Christ, as our Bodies are with the Bread and Wine.*[2]

We are reminded again of the stories we have read of God's invitation to all people.

In Holy Communion each one of us is invited to God's Holy Table. This is a feast for which we all have an open and regular invitation. It is a foretaste of the great banquet. We are reminded that it is an international banquet, as we think of our brothers and sisters partaking in Holy Communion across the world today, some where the burning sun is scorching the ground, others where snow and ice lie thickly, some gathering in grand and glorious buildings, others seated on grass under a tree. But the bread and the wine are the same, and by the Holy Spirit we all recognize Christ by faith as we eat and drink these Holy Gifts for God's Holy People.

The Holy Communion Service, as a Remembrance of the Last Supper of the Lord, helps us to take part in that relationship with Jesus Christ that the disciples shared, before his sacrifice that brought us life. As we read on Monday, Jesus had told the disciples, 'I am the bread of life'.

The Apostle Luke tells us that at his last supper on earth,

'How I have longed to eat this Passover with you before my death! [16]For I tell you, never again shall I eat it until the time when it finds its fulfilment in the kingdom of God.' [17]Then he took a cup, and after giving thanks he

2 *An Apology, or Answer in defence of the Church of England* (1562). Translated into English by Tho. Chayne (ed), For the Parker Society by John Ayre (The University Press: Cambridge, 1649).

said, 'Take this and share it among yourselves; [18]for I tell
you, from this moment I shall not drink the fruit of the
vine until the time when the kingdom of God comes.'
[19]Then he took bread, and after giving thanks he broke
it, and gave it to them with the words: 'This is my body.'
(Luke 22.15b–19)

A day later he died on the cross.

We remember and we give thanks for the bread of
life which was given for us, given to us, to feed us and
build us up. We remember and give thanks for the blood
issuing from the true 'vine of heaven', as the hymn writer
describes Christ's life being poured out in offering for
our sins. In our communion services we eat and drink
for eternal life.

The presence of Christ is not limited to an ecclesiastical
environment and a correctly liturgical service.

In the gospels we read of Christ being present in
miraculous meals on the hillsides above Galilee, being
present also in the breaking of bread with the disciples
on the way to Emmaus, in the breakfast on the beach by
the sea of Tiberius. For every follower of Jesus Christ,
every meal remembers his presence at their table. The
Communion Table and the dinner table and the picnic on
the seashore or the hillside are all alike in that at all of
them, by faith, Jesus Christ is the unseen guest. Yet at the
Communion Table *he is also the Host.* Here we taste and
touch and handle the Bread and Wine of the Kingdom,
and so from Betrayal Thursday till now, the Communion
Table when bread and wine are blessed in remembrance of
him is his table. And the Host invites all who are baptized
in his Death and Resurrection to come and partake, as

often as they can, 'proclaiming the death of the Lord until he comes' (1 Corinthians 11.23–26).

The Christian gospel would be a poor thing if Christ were confined to churches. Christ has broken every bound and we can find him anywhere in a Christ-filled world. When we have met him at the Communion Table, we are called to go out to meet him everywhere and serve Him in His world.

Jesus offers himself as Bread from heaven that satisfies completely and leads to eternal life. In John (6.53–58), he tells his listeners,

> In very truth I tell you, unless you eat the flesh of the Son of Man and drink his blood you can have no life in you. [54]Whoever eats my flesh and drinks my blood has eternal life, and I will raise him up on the last day. [55]My flesh is real food; my blood is real drink. [56]Whoever eats my flesh and drinks my blood dwells in me and I in him. [57]As the living Father sent me, and I live because of the Father, so whoever eats me will live because of me. [58]This is the bread which came down from heaven; it is not like the bread which our fathers ate; they are dead, but whoever eats this bread will live for ever.

Now we can see what Jesus is saying, 'You must drink my blood – you must take my life into every centre of your being – and that life of mine is the life which belongs to God.' By doing this we will be healed and renewed and, as Josiah Conder wrote in this hymn, we will be 'rooted, grafted and built in Christ'.

When we meet together in church and at home, we recall the Lord's Supper – there we know the divine action in Jesus Christ, which theology interprets and re-interprets continuously: *thanksgiving, proclamation, unity, assurance, memory of what Jesus Christ did for us,* invites us in *his presence* to encounter him and experience him. As Bishop John Jewel put it illuminatingly and in an insightful way:

> In this supper lieth a hidden mystery. There is the horror of sin, there is the death of our Lord for our sin represented, how he was wounded for our sins, and tormented for our iniquities, and led as a lamb to the slaughter. There may we see the shame of the cross, the darkness over the world, the earth to quake, the stones to cleave asunder, the graves to open, and the dead to rise. These things may we see in the supper: this is the meaning of these holy mysteries.[3]

Prayer

Jesus said, 'I came that they may have life and have it abundantly'. Lord Jesus, I thank you that you have called me to newness of life and you feed me and sustain me by your Body and Blood in the power of the Holy Spirit. Fill me afresh with your Spirit as I go out into your world and tell others that I am the empty-handed, hungry follower of Jesus, who has found Bread. Amen.

---

3 John Jowel, *A Treatise of the Sacraments, works of Bishop Jewel,* ed. J. Ayre (Cambridge: Parker Society, 1847), pp. 1123. See also Rowan Williams, *John Jewel 1522-1571, Treatise of the Sacraments* (1583) [a digest of his sermons] in *Love's Redeeming work, The Anglican Quest for Holiness,* Rowell, Stevenson, Williams (Oxford University Press: Oxford, 2001), pp. 68–74.

Reflection

Meditate on the Sacrament of Holy Communion. Remember Christ's words at the Last Supper – how might Holy Communion be expected to 'Feed us up'? As you sit at your table to eat, remember that Jesus is the unseen guest who is forever present. Invite friends of Jesus to your table – especially the poor, the prisoner, the differently-wired, because of their disabilities but who carry the same image and likeness of God, and those who are broken by our common disobedience.

WEEK 4: GROW UP!

Fourth Sunday of Advent: Grow Up and Be Ready

God our redeemer, who prepared the Blessed Virgin Mary to be the mother of your Son: grant that, as she looked for his coming as our Saviour, so we may be ready to greet him when he comes again as our Judge; who is alive and reigns with you, in the unity of the Holy Spirit, one God, now and for ever.

In *Wake Up to Advent!*, up to today, we have been looking at how we prepare for the coming of our Lord Jesus Christ – the preparations that preceded that First Advent, and the preparations we need for his Second Coming. We have awoken to Christ's new Light, we have examined our hearts and our actions and repented of all of our uncleannesses, pollution and shame. We have fed on the goodness of God's Word. We have fed on the Bread of Heaven. We are led to acknowledge our transience, vulnerability and creatureliness – though wonderfully created and fearfully made, loved and a source of delight to God our Father. We are maturing and growing in holiness, wisdom, insight and grace.

We also need to wake up to how the First Advent relates to the coming of Jesus Christ to our lives through the Holy Spirit – and how both of them relate to his coming to the world at the end of history.

Mary, after all, is not merely an example of preparing for Christ, not even the first example. She was called to prepare for the definitive coming, the incarnation of the Son of God, the fulfilment of the covenant. So every time I look for his coming afresh in my life, I do so because of what was done for and through Mary at that definitive moment. Every time I sigh and pray for the fulfilment of his coming before the whole world I look forward to the completion of what was begun for and through Mary.

This is difficult to say well because it is the Lord Jesus, not his mother, who is our model of obedient life before the Father. Still, since we cannot follow him unless we first look for his coming and receive him, we are also put in a position where we have to be like Mary, who had to prepare for him without all that we have in the way of knowledge about him. She is our model for this simple preparatory act of faith in God's promise – which is what you and I (and Advent itself!) want us to focus on.

This week, as the nativity of our Lord approaches in our yearly remembrance, we are looking at the way the Virgin Mary grew up – and grew up very quickly. As our Collect says, 'God had prepared her for the blessed calling of being the God-bearer, the mother of his Son, our redeemer'. We too are called to be ready as temples of the Holy Spirit, in the witness of our lives and words, so that we are ready to receive him when he comes again in glory. So, let us look to the example of his Blessed Mother, Mary, as she responded to this call to receive him.

In the sixth month the angel Gabriel was sent by God to Nazareth, a town in Galilee, [27]with a message for a girl betrothed to a man named Joseph, a descendant of David; the girl's name was Mary. [28]The angel went in and said to her, 'Greetings, most favoured one! The Lord is with you.' [29]But she was deeply troubled by what he said, and wondered what this greeting could mean. [30]Then the angel said to her, 'Do not be afraid, Mary, for God has been gracious to you; [31]you will conceive and give birth to a son, and you are to give him the name Jesus. [32]He will be great, and will be called Son of the Most High. The Lord God will give him the throne of his ancestor David, [33]and he will be king over Israel for ever; his reign shall never end.' [34]'How can this be?' said Mary. 'I am still a virgin'. [35]The angel answered, 'The Holy Spirit will come upon you, and the power of the Most High will overshadow you; for that reason the holy child to be born will be called Son of God. [36]Moreover your kinswoman Elizabeth has herself conceived a son in her old age; and she who is reputed barren is now in her sixth month, [37]for God's promises can never fail.' [38]'I am the Lord's servant,' said Mary; 'may it be as you have said.' Then the angel left her. (Luke 1.26–38)

Here, in this familiar passage of great wonder, we meet the girl, Mary, for the first time. Who was she? She was a girl, living in the town of Nazareth in Galilee (a small northern town), betrothed and soon to be married. Not an unusual story; but she was visited by an angel – the angel Gabriel, no less, with a life-changing message. She was 'favoured' by God, Gabriel told her. We, along with Mary, might well wonder what 'being favoured' by God would mean for her. Mary didn't know. She was still unawakened to the realization of what it would all mean, what the angel was leading up to. We know though what happens next. We know that when the angel explained how that 'favour' would work out, it would mean, in the first instance, that she would be pregnant out of wedlock, that she would probably have to face censure and condemnation from her betrothed, and from her family. It would mean she would have the responsibility of bringing up the Son of God; that she would see him court danger and hostility in his ministry; and that finally she would see him die in agony as a criminal. That scenario isn't what we normally think of when we talk of someone being particularly 'favoured'. The 'favour' wasn't that she'd be an honoured member of her community, contented and untroubled in her life. It was rather that she was chosen for a greater destiny than comfort or ease. She was chosen for *eternal favour*. Gabriel added, 'the Lord is with you.' Even in the future, when she felt most lonely and bewildered by the experiences in her life, the Lord would be with her.

She had found 'favour with God'! What was it about Mary that God should choose her for a vocation which would be full of challenges to her character, her courage, her faith, her wisdom? God knew who Mary was, he knew her strengths and her potential, just as he knows each one of us. He knew that she had the virtues which would help her through all the trials, all the joys and sorrows that were to come.

The Blessed Virgin Mary looked with bewilderment at this strange visitation by the angel Gabriel. What did it mean, to have an angel come and greet her? Her reaction gives us a first clue to what kind of girl she was – her strength of mind and character, her resilience and trust in the God who makes the impossible possible.

She was young, but her mind was resilient. She was young but she would be steeped in the strong faith and religious knowledge of her people. God speaking through an angel was not unheard of. She didn't scream, or faint, or run away. She was troubled and puzzled, but she gives the angel's words serious thought. What did it all mean?

So she wondered – perhaps she even wondered aloud – 'What do you mean, what are you saying?'

So the angel Gabriel tells her. He does well to tell her not to be afraid, and to reassure her that the Lord means well for her, because it transpires that the purpose of his greeting is going to take her breath away. In three short packed sentences, the angel Gabriel sets out the whole of God's plan for the salvation of the world. She will have a baby called Jesus (a name meaning 'saviour', 'deliverer'). He will be the Son of God; he will be given the throne of David and therefore King over Israel and he will rule for ever.

Mary, understandably, picks up on the first statement, which is outside her community-lived experience. How can I have a baby? She is not afraid to question this astonishing announcement, and she responds with a practical objection. 'How is that going to work? I know how babies are conceived, and I'm a virgin!'

The angel Gabriel explains again – it will happen through the mystery and power of the Holy Spirit of God. And, to reassure Mary that it's not only possible, but that God has moved already six months ago with someone she knows, the angel Gabriel tells her the news about her cousin Elizabeth's pregnancy in her old age and barrenness. God is the God of life. And he can bring new life to both old age and innocent youth. 'God's promises never fail', says Gabriel.

We are not told how long Mary pondered these amazing revelations before she responded. Her mind must have been whirling, but her response was firm and committed. Mary was a girl of strong faith – 'I know the Lord', she says. 'I serve him. I'm ready to accept whatever he wills for me'.

And the angel Gabriel leaves her. He has said 'the Lord is with you', but Mary will need to grow in strength and faith in that promise as the difficult days come.

Prayer

Lord God of surprises, we thank you that you know each one of us and you call us to humble obedience to your will. Give us that readiness to hear, accept and follow your purposes for our lives. Amen.

Reflection

Think of the times when you feel God has asked you to take on daunting tasks.

Have you felt 'favoured' by God's calling you to these things?

Have you been ready, or reluctant to take them on?

Have you been aware of God's word assuring you of God's grace and faithfulness as you obey?

WEEK 4: MONDAY

Grow Up for Transformation and Hope (Magnificat: Luke 1.39–56)

[39]Soon afterwards Mary set out and hurried away to a town in the uplands of Judah. [40]She went into Zechariah's house and greeted Elizabeth. [41]And when Elizabeth heard Mary's greeting, the baby stirred in her womb. Then Elizabeth was filled with the Holy Spirit, [42]and exclaimed in a loud voice, 'God's blessing is on you above all women, and his blessing

is on the fruit of your womb. [43]Who am I, that the mother of my Lord should visit me? [44]I tell you, when your greeting sounded in my ears, the baby in my womb leapt for joy. [45]Happy is she who has had faith that the Lord's promise to her would be fulfilled!'

[46]And Mary said: 'My soul tells out the greatness of the Lord, [47]my spirit has rejoiced in God my Saviour; [48]for he has looked with favour on his servant, lowly as she is. From this day forward all generations will count me blessed, [49]for the Mighty God has done great things for me. His name is holy, [50]his mercy sure from generation to generation toward those who fear him. [51]He has shown the might of his arm, he has routed the proud and all their schemes; [52]he has brought down monarchs from their thrones, and raised on high the lowly. [53]He has filled the hungry with good things, and sent the rich away empty. [54-55]He has come to the help of Israel his servant, as he promised to our forefathers; he has not forgotten to show mercy to Abraham and his children's children for ever.' [56]Mary stayed with Elizabeth about three months and then returned home.

Mary had just received a life-changing message from an angel. She was to be the mother of God's Son. While her mind was in turmoil – busy trying to process the fact that she had 'found favour with God who was gracious to her' and that she was going to be pregnant and have a baby who would be a King, a Saviour – the practical aspect of her character that we saw yesterday would also be thinking, 'What's the next step for me now? Mother would be the obvious person to help, but I can't tell her this yet. I certainly can't tell Joseph until I'm quite sure what's happening and how I'm going to cope.' The memory of that visitation would be going round and round in her mind, and she would remember the last startling statement the angel told her at the end of all the other amazing things. She wasn't alone in this miracle: 'Moreover your kinswoman Elizabeth has herself conceived a son in her old age; and she who is reputed barren is now in her sixth month.'

How marvellous is God's grace always going before us. As Bishop David Jenkins of Durham used to say to anyone called to ministry, 'If you feel you are not up to it, God is already down to it. And for God's sake do not be religious; And for the sake of the world, be holy.' God has given Mary and Elizabeth to each other so that they can share their joy and hope as well as their confusion. No wonder Mary hurries away to Elizabeth. She is a young woman of action and decision. She may be young and the journey may take several days on foot, but she is strong in mind and body and she is ready to go alone to discover what God has done already, and will do in her. God has already worked a miracle for Elizabeth and she has had six months to come to terms with it. She will know how it feels, and together they can share an experience which no one else would quite understand. How wonderful is God's grace always going before us.

As soon as Elizabeth hears Mary's voice, the baby leapt in her womb for joy – it was as if the Holy Spirit was bearing witness to the God-given life growing in Elizabeth and which will grow in Mary. The six month's John, in Elizabeth's womb, was greeting the promised Son of God to grow in Mary's womb.

God's purposes are being worked out through the very simplest and most unlikely people. Elizabeth is a priest's wife, if you like, living in a rather out-of-the-way place in the hill country of Judah. Mary is a very young, unmarried girl living in an unremarkable little town in the country, engaged to marry a carpenter. These two apparently down-to-earth women celebrate together the wonder and mystery of God's action. Mary sings for joy. And what a song! She sings a song about the glory of God, about his power and graciousness, but her song is also a song about her people, about the history of God's love and about the promise of justice and transformation. That God is acting now to usher in his Rule of Justice in which his people will 'do justice, love kindness, and walk humbly with their God' (Micah 6.8). Putting the present world order upside down. Living today as if tomorrow is already here.

The people of Israel in the time of Christ were suffering – as were the people in Micah's time. They were oppressed by having an occupying foreign force in their land, by corruption and abuse of power from their officials, and by the dishonesty of many of their religious leaders. Mary's song recognizes that God is promising to change all this: he will bring mercy for the humble, justice and reversal for those who have misused their power; peace, plenty for the poor and the mistreated. It is quite a transfiguring and glorifying song – as is fitting for the celebration of the promise of the Saviour who makes all things new!

In this song we see that Mary is a girl whose deep wisdom and compassion recognizes the injustices of the world. She sees clearly the longing of her people for freedom, and she speaks with a mature understanding of how God's love and justice and mercy had always been present in his promises through the ages. She lifts her voice in praise and wonder to glorify God's faithfulness and the hope of his promises. This is a song of astonished exultation as she begins to see the role she is called upon to fulfil.

Has Mary found favour with God because he has seen in her the potential for the understanding and compassion for others that she will show as she loves and nurtures Jesus? Did God choose her because she is a girl who will surround Jesus with her God-given understanding of justice and mercy? Did God recognize that she would be a wonderful pattern of humble obedience and trust in God's promises? As she grew and matured into the servant of God she was created to be, all these gifts would be used in his service.

Mary remained with Elizabeth for three months. She would have observed Zechariah's inability to speak until he announced his son's name after the birth. She would have celebrated with them the promise and hope for the future. She would have gained strength and comfort from knowing that it was indeed God who called her and would equip her for all that she had to face. And she would have grown in courage and confidence so that she could return home to face whatever incredulity, anger or condemnation might be awaiting her. God was in charge. This was his enterprise put into the hands of a fallible young girl. How trusting! God believes in us more than we believe in him. He trusts us even more on the ground of our defeat and failure, just as he trusted the Apostle Peter by another charcoal fire, calling him again 'Come, follow me'. 'Peter do you love me? Do you really love me? Am I really your friend?' (John 21.15–19)

Prayer

Lord of power and justice, grant us hearts of compassion to look upon your suffering world and remember with thankful hearts the great things you have done. When we need to know your hope, help us to recall your promise to strengthen us, to save us, to be with us, and to raise us up.

Reflection

Think about the times when you have found that a friend has experienced God moving in their life in the same way you have – either through events or prayers which coincide.

How have you responded to these signs of God's grace?

How can you relate them to God's action through the ages?

Have they made you more expectant that God will speak and act?

Have they made you more ready to respond to his call?

WEEK 4: CHRISTMAS EVE

Grow Up in Endurance and Courage (Luke 2.1–7)

In those days a decree was issued by the emperor Augustus for a census to be taken throughout the Roman world. ²This was the first registration of its kind; it took place when Quirinius was governor of Syria. ³Everyone made his way to his own town to be registered. ⁴⁻⁵Joseph went up to Judaea from the town of Nazareth in Galilee, to register in the city of David called Bethlehem, because he was of the house of

David by descent; and with him went Mary, his betrothed, who was expecting her child. [6]While they were there the time came for her to have her baby, [7]and she gave birth to a son, her firstborn. She wrapped him in swaddling clothes, and laid him in a manger, because there was no room for them at the inn.

Around six months later, Mary was once again making a journey. This was very different from the initial excitement, wonder and possibly a little trepidation which sent her 'hurrying to visit Elizabeth'. This time she was far on in her pregnancy and much had happened in between.

The disclosure of her pregnancy and conversation with Joseph about the angel and her conceiving of the Son of God must have been painful. The silence and the waiting, while he pondered how to react, would have tested her courage and faith. Would Joseph denounce her for unfaithfulness and leave her to the public punishment of the crowd? Even if he decided to break off the engagement quietly she would have been left alone without support as she raised an illegitimate baby without a human father. What? An alien?

Once again, as we read in Matthew (1.19–21), God is with her, as he promised, and in Matthew we see that he is also with Joseph. Joseph was a just man, and he struggled with his conscience about how he should respond to Mary's news. He was a thoughtful, merciful man faced with what he saw as a moral dilemma which needed action of some kind.

Like many of us, Joseph probably went to bed tormented by an unresolved problem. Yet God does not abandon us. His angel appeared and spoke to Joseph, encouraging him in his inclination to mercy, and confirming what Mary had told him. God graciously settled his doubts about Mary's faithfulness and purity, and gave him the strength both to be able to accept her, and to counter any reaction from family or neighbours. As with Zechariah, the coming of the angel graciously made God's purposes clear to a doubting mind.

Once again, we see that the lives of ordinary people can find favour with God. Joseph, a carpenter, is called to be the earthly father of God's Son, and God meets with him and equips him for the task.

Now, when it becomes clear that Joseph will have to go away for some time to register for the census, Mary elects to go with him, even though she must be close to giving birth. The appearance of the angel to Joseph has created a closer bond between them. As with her cousin Elizabeth, the shared experience of God's direct action gives them a common mind and purpose for their lives which no ordinary marriage ceremony would provide.

We aren't told about the response of her parents, and we hear nothing in Scripture of the reaction of her neighbours and friends; but Joseph has accepted her, and that is all that was needed. She will, in time to come, have plenty of experience of criticism and condemnation relating to her son, but with God's presence to guide and comfort she will endure.

So they set off on a journey of about 80 miles, a journey of several days on foot. They are taking the road to an unknown future. They set off to Joseph's home town, Bethlehem, the town of the great King David, whose throne, God has told them, their baby would one day take.

It would have been a wearisome journey, but we have

seen that Mary is not daunted by travelling. She had hurried a similar distance to visit Elizabeth early in her pregnancy, and the same distance home three months later. Now, though, her pregnancy is further advanced, and the way would have been tiring, but we have learned that Mary is a young woman of courage and in this reading we begin to recognize the strength of her endurance also.

Much later, Jesus would tell his would-be followers in Luke (9.62), 'No one who sets his hand to the plough and then looks back is fit for the kingdom of God.' Mary had already accepted this kind of commitment when she first spoke to the angel Gabriel. She had the 'stickability' which would be needed for the rest of her life.

Verses 6 and 7 of Luke Chapter 2 tell us, '⁶While they were there the time came for her to have her baby, ⁷and she gave birth to a son, her firstborn.' What a simple statement of a momentous event. In these days of birthing suites and highly sophisticated medical technology and care it is sometimes difficult to remember what unaided birth was like. There is no mention in the Gospels of Matthew and Luke of family or extended family helping with the birth. It may well have been difficult and exhausting, but anyone who has given birth will know the exhilaration and wonder of holding that new life. Mary wrapped him up and laid him in a feeding trough in the animal quarters of the place they had found to stay. 'The Son of God had emptied himself of his glory and power to come to earth. Emmanuel, God with us.' As St Paul says in 2 Corinthians (8.9), 'He was rich, yet for your sakes he became poor, so you through his poverty might become rich.'

The reason Jesus – God with us, Emmanuel, Saviour – was born in such a poor, humble circumstance was for our sake. He did this because His indomitable love reached out to do for humankind what humankind could not do for itself.

Looking at her baby as he lay in the manger, a cattle's feeding and drinking trough, Mary must have been full of wonder in the knowledge that here lay the Son of God, vulnerable and dependent – given into her care to love and nurture.

Mary had grown up a lot in the last nine months. Nine months earlier she was living the life of a simple small-town girl, with nothing more significant in view for her future than her wedding to a man her parents thought suitable for her. Since then, she has experienced God's direct and powerful action in her life, and in the lives of those close to her. For nine months she has carried God's son in her womb, and as he grew, so her understanding of what she had been called upon to do would have grown stronger.

New parents will often tell you that it isn't until they look at their new baby that they realize the fullness of what love means, and how much their own parents must have loved them. Mary would have recognized in that moment, not only her own overwhelming protective love for Jesus, but how much more God loves us, people wonderfully created and beautifully made in his image and likeness.

Prayer

Christmas Eve Collect
Almighty God, you make us glad with the yearly remembrance of the birth of your Son Jesus Christ: grant that, as we joyfully receive him as our redeemer, so we may with sure confidence behold him when he shall come

to be our judge; who is alive and reigns with you, in the unity of the Holy Spirit, one God, now and for ever. Amen.

Reflection

Spend some time thinking again about how Jesus came into the world. On one level, this is a very simple story. Consider the simple things that make each day special in your life.

Think again of your Christmas preparations, and look for the simple things that you hope will bring joy in the coming days.

Consider the things that Mary is pondering as she looks at the Son of God sleeping in the manger. What are we called to do, in our service of the newborn King?

WEEK 4: CHRISTMAS DAY

'Hark! the Herald Angels Sing' (Luke 2.8–20)

[8]Now in this same district there were shepherds out in the fields, keeping watch through the night over their flock. [9]Suddenly an angel of the Lord appeared to them, and the glory of the Lord shone round them. They were terrified, [10]but the angel said, 'Do not be afraid; I bring you good news, news of great joy for the whole nation. [11]Today there has been born to you in the city of David, a deliverer – the Messiah, the Lord. [12]This will be the sign for you: you will find a baby wrapped in swaddling clothes, and lying in a manger.' [13]All at once there was with the angel, a great company of the heavenly host, singing praise to God: [14]'Glory to God in the highest heaven, and on earth peace to all in whom he delights.'

> ¹⁵After the angels had left them and returned to heaven the shepherds said to one another, 'Come, let us go straight to Bethlehem and see this thing that has happened, which the Lord has made known to us.' ¹⁶They hurried off and found Mary and Joseph and the baby lying in the manger. ¹⁷When they saw the child, they related what they had been told about him; ¹⁸and all who heard were astonished at what the shepherds said. ¹⁹But Mary treasured up all these things and pondered over them. ²⁰The shepherds returned glorifying and praising God for what they had heard and seen; it had all happened as they had been told.

This picture of the simplicity of the newborn Christ Child lying in a manger, a cattle's feeding and drinking trough, remains with us as the focus moves to a dark hillside. Suddenly the night's deep darkness is torn apart by glorious heavenly light as once again an angel appears to earthly people.

Heaven's response is full of glory and exuberant joy – a festal shout of joy shared with shepherds. The powerful fear and reject Jesus Christ's coming, the powerless and humble see and worship. Just as Mary foresaw in her song of God's Glory, the Magnificat, God's gift would be to raise up those who are and have 'nothing'.

In yesterday's reading we saw how Jesus Christ emptied himself to come down to share the lives of even the humblest person. Shepherds were certainly among the humblest – at the bottom of the pile in terms of social status. Shepherds found it hard to maintain religious purity as defined by Jewish tradition. They couldn't keep the Sabbath because sheep need constant protection. They spent most of their time in the fields away from society and had no strength or influence in community. They were in the lower classes of society, unnoticed or looked down on by those in power.

Yet God's favour was on the shepherds, just as it had been on Zechariah and Elizabeth; just as it had shone on Mary, and on Joseph. The glorious news of the Messiah's birth was announced to shepherds because, as the Apostle Paul tells us in 1 Corinthians (1.27–29), 'Yet, to shame the wise, God has chosen what the world counts as folly, and to shame what is strong, God has chosen what the world counts weakness. He has chosen things without rank or standing in the world, mere nothings, to overthrow the existing order. So no place is left for any human pride in the presence of God'. Because God had already promised through the Prophet Isaiah, 'The Lord has anointed me; he has sent me to announce good news to the humble' (Isaiah 61.1b) – wonderful words, later repeated and 'fulfilled in the presence of the people' by Jesus in the Synagogue at Nazareth.

The angels brought the good news for 'the whole nation'. No one was to be missed out. We were all to be assured that, however low we are, God in Jesus Christ wants to share his good news with us.

The angels also brought this news to the shepherds so that, through them, Mary and Joseph would hear how Heaven was affirming the truth of his birth, and rejoicing with them in the fulfilment of God's promises.

Mary is a young woman of prayer, patient humility, as well as someone who has courage, endurance and resilience. As she ponders the shepherd's story of the angels' message and takes in the wonderful knowledge that heaven itself is rejoicing with her, she grows in the deep motherly understanding of all that will be required from her. She is surrounded by a cloud of witnesses rooting for her.

During this last week, we have been focusing on Mary, the mother of Jesus Christ, and her growth through humility, obedience, courage and hope. But it is appropriate that today we also focus on the angels, who have been part of the story this week. Each day these messengers of God have been accompanying and guiding our characters with gentleness and love. And finally they are part of the great heavenly outpouring of joy as they recount the story of God's amazing Love.

So let us join together with the angels as we celebrate God's amazing grace, and with hearts full of joy welcome the Advent of our King. Many of us will be singing this glorious carol today in our churches – it is my favourite of all the carols because it is an amazing, jubilant and joyful welcome 'to the new born King'. A mere three verses tell the whole story of God's Love in Jesus Christ. And Sir David Willcocks's descant has the sopranos enjoying much fun in the third verse. It brings the great words alive.

1 Hark! the herald angels sing
   glory to the new-born King,
peace on earth and mercy mild,
   God and sinners reconciled.
Joyful, all ye nations rise,
   Join the triumph of the skies;
with the angelic host proclaim,
   'Christ is born in Bethlehem.'
Hark, the herald angels sing
glory to the new-born King.

127

2 Christ, by highest heaven adored.
  Christ, the everlasting Lord,
late in time behold him come,
  Offspring of a Virgin's womb!
Veiled in flesh the Godhead see:
  Hail, the incarnate Deity,
pleased as man with man to dwell,
  Jesus, our Emmanuel.
Hark, the herald angels sing
  glory to the new-born King.

3 Hail, the heav'n-born Prince of Peace!
  Hail, the Sun of Righteousness!
Light and life to all he brings,
  risen with healing in his wings.
Mild he lays his glory by,
  born that man no more may die,
born to raise the sons of earth,
  born to give them second birth.
Hark, the herald angels sing
  glory to the new-born King.

Charles Wesley (1707–1788)

As we have journeyed through Advent, we have learned of how, in God's love story with human beings, our Heavenly Father has always been calling his beloved children, lost in the wilderness of this world and its confusion, to *Wake Up, Clean Up, Feed Up* and *Grow Up* into his image and likeness.

Today, we *Wake Up* to the glorious news of the Light of God coming into the darkness of his world. He has come to show us how to *Clean Up* by turning to him, and

'HARK! THE HERALD ANGELS SING' (LUKE 2.8–20)

laying all our 'uncleannesses' at his feet. He has come to *Feed* us with the Living Word, and the Bread of Life. And, filled with the glory of his coming, and filled with the hope of eternal life with him, we know we will *Grow Up* in him too 'so shall we fully grow up into Christ' (Ephesians 4.15b).

Prayer – Collect for Christmas Day

Almighty God, you have given us your only-begotten Son
to take our nature upon him and as at this time to be born
of a pure virgin: grant that we, who have been born again
and made your children by adoption and grace, may daily
be renewed by your Holy Spirit;
through Jesus Christ your Son our Lord,
who is alive and reigns with you,
in the unity of the Holy Spirit,
one God, now and for ever. Amen.

Reflection

As we rejoice with friends and family today in our churches
and our homes, reflect on how God speaks to each one of
us:

• through the light he brings to our minds and lives;
• through his promise to cleanse us from sin;
• through his Living Word in Scripture;
• through our feeding on the Bread of Heaven;
• through his guidance and nurturing as we grow ever closer to him;
• through the heavenly glory of worship and celebration.

WEEK 4: CHRISTMAS DAY

Think about ways in which we can encourage those we meet to *Wake Up*, *Clean Up*, *Feed Up* and *Grow Up*. Rejoice, our Redeemer has come to us and to all the people. And he will come again in glory. Alleluia! Amen!